O

Ruwenzori Range

Fort Portal

T O R O

KAMPALA

Lake George

U G A N D A

Entebbe

A N K O L E

Mbarara

Bweranyangi

KIGEZI

Kisiizi

Lake

Mira Mts

Mt Muhabura

Kabale

Lake Bunyoni

Victoria

R W A N D A

Ruhengeri

ra

Lake Muhazi

N

KIGALI

Gahini

yogwe

BUGESERA

Maranyundo

R. Kagera

Nyabara

Butare

Buye

Akanyaru

Ngozi

Buhiga

B U R U N D I

R. Ruvuvu

T A N Z A N I A

Gitega

N

W — E

Matana

Source
of Nile

S

Miles 20 10   0   20   40   60

Joan Rundell

Breath of Life

A land of hills and valleys . . .
a land which the Lord thy God careth for

DEUTERONOMY 11: 11, 12

PATRICIA ST JOHN

*

BREATH OF LIFE

The Story of the Ruanda Mission

*

WITH A FOREWORD BY
THE ARCHBISHOP OF YORK

THE NORFOLK PRESS
19 Draycott Place
London SW3

First published in England 1971
by the Norfolk Press

Copyright © by the Ruanda Mission C.M.S. 1971
St Mark's Church, Kennington Park Road,
London, S.E.11

ISBN 0 85211 004 9

Printed in England by
Latimer Trend & Co Ltd
Plymouth

Foreword

In 1955 I had the privilege of visiting some of the places mentioned in this book. I have had the greater privilege of knowing some of the people who feature in it. For these reasons alone I am glad to write a Foreword to *Breath of Life*.

But I welcome this opportunity for another reason: the story told here is a very remarkable one. A period of only half a century is covered—a very short time in the long story of the Church—and yet what astonishing progress in evangelism is recorded!

I hope that many will read this book and ponder it carefully, not only studying it as a piece of twentieth-century Church history, but also asking such questions as these: What has the growth of this young Church, and the movement of the Spirit within it, to say to the older Churches, steeped in history and convention and set in their ways? Has the Church in Ruanda been given certain insights which to us have become dim? What is the Spirit saying to *our* Church through this story?

No doubt new problems will face the Church in Ruanda in the coming years—the problems of maturity differ from those of youth and adolescence—and those who guide its destiny will need new gifts of the Spirit to discern the issues that are at stake. The readers of this deeply interesting story of the Church in Ruanda will pray that its members will continue to put first their zeal for the Name that is above every name.

DONALD EBOR:

Bishopthorpe
York

Contents

Illustrations

Introduction

BY THE REV FESTO KIVENGERE B.D.

It is with a deep sense of gratitude to God that I write these introductory remarks to the story of what He has done in the last fifty years through ordinary men and women such as those who constitute the Ruanda Mission.

St Paul says: "When the necessary time reached completion God sent His Son, born of a woman." As one to whom God sent the Good News of His Son through His messengers of the Ruanda Mission, I can look back to what the spiritual as well as the physical aspects of our life were like when the message of God's love reached our people. And I can say that the necessary time for preparing us for that message had certainly reached completion.

In our religious life we were always striving to appease the distant, forbidding Creator from whom we sought desperately for security. The only possible relationship with this Creator seemed to be through the medium-spirits of our ancestors. We hoped that these would plead our cause, convince Him of our worthiness, and bring us the security for which we longed. This longing made our people redouble their efforts to find ways and means of appeasing the spirits but we never received the assurance we were seeking. We were haunted by a terrible sense of uncertainty.

But the same God who commanded light to shine out of darkness sent His light to shine in our hearts and minds, illuminating them with "the knowledge of the glory of God, seen in the face of Jesus Christ". The compelling love of God, who had seen our futile efforts to achieve a right relationship with Him, sent the founders of the Ruanda Mission to our land. Their aim was to tell us how much God loved us. Because of the strange colour of their skin, their strange language, their strange way of doing things and their human weaknesses, the apparently simple task of communication would have been impossible through human techniques alone. It could have ended in a confusion of tongues like that of Babel. It needed the Spirit of God, the Spirit of life and order, the mighty wind which swept over the chaotic surface of the dark waters before creation, to breathe over the efforts of the Ruanda Mission and our own attempts to understand what it was all about.

Slowly but steadily we caught sight of the fact that the God we had sought without finding, had always been seeking us. We began to realize that He cared so much about our whole lives that He gave His Son to suffer for us and to bring us into that right relationship with Him. Jesus and His love became the only power able to draw us from our own deep despair into the glorious hope of the Gospel.

Through the years, a threefold approach was used to meet the needs of the whole man: the proclamation of the Good News to touch our hearts, the teaching of the mind, and the healing of the body. Churches, schools and hospitals sprang up in many places and thousands flocked to them. Yet something was missing. So often there was a general assent to the new teaching but little real change in people's lives.

Then—nearly twenty years after the founding of the Mission —that same Spirit came in new power. The Spirit which had created the longing in our hearts, swept through us—congregations and missionaries alike—in another Pentecost. Silence gave way to praise; there was glory in the faces of those who responded to the life-giving Spirit. Barriers between brethren broke down in the presence of the risen Christ. Men and women entered into the liberating power of Christ's cross. I for one can never thank God enough; not only for what He did among my own people but also in my own life when it pleased Him to come to my rescue. He turned me from my traditional darkness of sin and despair and set my imprisoned life free. He brought me back to Himself, removed my barriers of resistance and pronounced me forgiven through His precious blood.

The extent of what God has done in our countries through the Ruanda Mission will only be fully known in eternity. The echoes of praise from lives set free by God's redeeming love in Christ will continue to be heard through the ages to come. The deep effect of the message given by the Mission, and now being proclaimed by those of us who received it, can be seen in many profound changes in our communities, in our home life, and in one of the most spectacular movements of the Christian faith in any society.

May this movement of God's Spirit continue in the young Churches and in the Mission itself, among its missionaries and its supporters at home. May this story of how the Holy Spirit can work through ordinary people inspire readers by the same Spirit. May it encourage them to tell the story to our world of the seventies, and point confused souls out of the smog of modern heathenism to the living Christ.

The Rev Festo Kivengere B.D. was educated in Ruanda Mission schools. He trained as a teacher at Mukono College, Uganda, and taught at the Alliance High School in Dodoma, Tanzania. After two years' study in the U.S.A. he received the degree of Bachelor of Divinity and is now a travelling evangelist, answering calls from every continent. On a number of occasions he has been a member of the Billy Graham team.

Summary of Principal Events

Summary of Principal Events

1

The Seed

Where did it start? If "the blood of the martyrs is the seed of the Church", then East African territory is a field richly sown. In 1670 a hundred and forty Portuguese and Africans refused to become Moslems and died for their faith at Mombasa, and just over two hundred years later Shergold Smith and O'Neill, the vanguard of the Church Missionary Society (C.M.S.), preached the Gospel for a year in the hills and forests of Uganda and were eventually killed in Tanganyika. They saw little result, but they handed on the torch to Mackay and Wilson, and one by one Africans turned to the Light and the Church was born in Uganda.

"Tell the King I die for Uganda," said Hannington as he knelt for his execution, and he did not die in vain, for many followed his example, and a year later a crowd of martyrs, Protestant and Catholic, went home to God. They were mostly very young, these first believers who endured death so steadfastly. The youngest who dared the flames was a child of eleven years old. "You, who have seen us, go and tell our brothers that we have broken Satan's chains," they said in the face of torture, and the Word was passed on, as all over the land men were set free from the prison of bondage to witchcraft and heathenism.

Dawn had broken and no power could turn it back. Twelve years later Pilkington was struck down, but before he died revival had swept the land, and he had left his legacy in the hands of the Baganda (the people of Uganda)—the Bible in their own language.

Four years later, in a land very far from Uganda, a young Norwegian mother died. She was the wife of Dr Stanley Smith, one of the Cambridge Seven who went out with a group to China under the leadership of Hudson Taylor, and she left a year-old baby called Algernon. The broken-hearted father, absorbed in the task of evangelizing a vast province, sent his little son to boarding school as soon as possible, and later took him home to England; a small, fair, shy child, pathetically anxious to please everybody. No close relatives seem to have been available, but two maiden ladies, the Misses Watney, offered to make a home for him in Croydon and to be responsible for his schooling.

The ladies were up to the eyes in church and parish work, and the situation cannot have been easy for them or for Algie, but both parties did their best. They sent him to Winchester College, provided holiday tutors, taught him the Bible and prayed for him. And he on his side, truly grateful for their kindness, tried hard to please, dutifully learning his daily scripture portions, accompanying them to meetings and dreaming through long sermons; but it was always a relief to put off this polite mask of piety and plunge back into school life. Winchester was like most other public schools of that time, but some innate streak of cleanliness and horror of bestiality kept him aloof from the evil around him, and the influence of his father's long, loving letters was strong too.

His early school days passed uneventfully and contentedly, with as much football and cricket, and as little work, as possible.

But his adolescent years were not without conflict. When he was fourteen he attended yet another meeting with the Misses Watney, but this time he did not dream. A Mr Ensor preached on the verse "Prepare to meet thy God" and the boy was moved. Those who wanted to accept Christ were asked to stand, and Algie, partly conscious of the ladies praying at his side, partly conscious of his spiritual need, stood up. But the moment of emotion passed and he was left to act out a conversion he had never really experienced. The happy Watney sisters praised God and arranged for him to undergo baptism by immersion, and he was interviewed and knew all the answers. It was unthinkable to disappoint his kind friends, so there was nothing to do but to acquiesce and he was baptized at their home church. It was one of the most miserable nights of his boyhood.

It was more of a relief than ever to get back to school and be himself, and yet there was a change. He started going to communion and attended the Christian Union regularly. His experience had been deep enough to make him restless, but not deep enough to leave any real mark on his daily life, and he was desperately shy of his friends knowing that he had turned religious. The arrival of his aunt at the railway station in a Salvation Army bonnet embarrassed him so acutely that he contrived to keep her down town until the whole school was out on the playing fields. Then he showed her round the empty buildings in a great hurry and did not breathe freely till the bonnet was borne away in the train.

The years rolled by and he left Winchester for the last time. Largely through the visit of Albert Cook, a pioneer doctor in Uganda, he had decided to study medicine and would be going up to Cambridge. It is always a solemn time for a youth when he leaves school for ever and starts afresh, a man in a wider world with far greater possibilities and scope for good or evil and, in September 1908, on the very eve of entering the university, Algie decided to stop compromising. It was not an emotional experience, rather a reasonable decision. He had always mentally believed in the love and sacrifice of Christ. Now he realized that the only honourable response to that love was to give up his life entirely to Christ's service and he made the supreme choice.

It was well for him as he stepped out, timid but decided, into his new life that he found himself in digs next door to

Leonard Sharp, just down from Harrow. They were very different characters and came from very different backgrounds. Algie had never known the security of a family, but Len was the second of six children, the child of a loving, brave, Christian mother, a strong, practical boy, a born leader with a charming smile that would suddenly soften the very determined lines of his face. The attraction probably lay in the discovery that both had given over their lives to Christ at the time of leaving school, and were both most earnestly seeking God's guidance for their futures. "So we formed a partnership in games and work that was surely according to the divine purpose," wrote one of them fifty years later. And that first term at Trinity they faced together the problem of the unevangelized world. One can well imagine them walking the Backs at Cambridge together in the autumn sunshine under the blaze of the dying leaves, but in their hearts was the gladness of a great new adventure. Daily they prayed together, "Lord, take us to some tribe that has never heard the Gospel before."

They had plenty of opportunity to hear for it was the heyday of missions, and men whose names have since become famous visited Cambridge frequently. The Christian Union of that time was a large gathering of dedicated young students, ripe for the inspiring influence of such men as John Mott, who challenged the student body to evangelize the world in their generation; C. T. Studd, who had led the Cambridge Seven to China; Barclay Buxton, founder of the Japanese Evangelistic Band; Karl Kumm with his vision of planting a chain of mission stations in Africa from West to East to stem the advance of Islam. Dr Albert Cook came, too, and Algie was delighted to see his old friend again. After his visit, the minds of the two young men turned increasingly towards East Africa.

In London, Len trained at St Thomas's, and Algie at St George's, but they still met frequently to talk and pray about the future, and the bond between them did not weaken. They had started out together on their Christian life and it seemed natural that they should go on together and that God would call them out to the same place, although they were still not sure where that place would be. They had both done well in their studies and England had everything to offer them, but that as yet unknown race, who had never heard the Gospel and for whom they had now prayed for six years, claimed them. When both were qualified in 1914, they decided to accept Dr Cook's offer and go out to work with him for a year at Mengo hospital in Uganda.

Few in the early months of 1914 believed that England would go to war. No cloud of apprehension had fallen over the privileged young gentlemen in the universities and hospitals. They made their plans as usual, but a few months later the storm had broken and the youth of England was caught up in a frenzy of patriotism. The entire staff of St George's Hospital went off to France, and Algie went with them. His natural tendency to go along with the crowd had not yet been entirely tempered by the love of God into that gentle, understanding tolerance and the ability to see all sides of a question that so characterized him later. He flung himself into life at the Front and within a year was twice mentioned in despatches and won the M.C. But God kept the reckless young life that had been so truly committed to Him, and brought him back safely. By the middle of 1915, his battalion was decimated and Mengo had become a base military hospital for the Uganda section of the East African forces. He lost no time in becoming engaged to Zoë Sharp, whom he had often met on his free week-ends from hospital. She was a quiet, home-loving girl and Len had always been her hero. If Len loved and trusted Algie, it was not hard for her to do the same. Then, with that urgent matter settled, he was drafted overseas to Mengo Hospital, where he rejoined Len, who had already been working there for about nine months.

Unmoved by the crowd, and against popular opinion, Len

had set his face steadfastly towards the land to which he believed God had called him and had arrived there in February 1915. He had been given a commission and had become medical officer to the Belgian troops, forming a relationship which stood him in good stead later on. Delighted to be together again, the two friends worked hard for the next three years, learning much from the wise doctor brothers, Albert and Jack Cook, who were so deeply loved and trusted by the Africans. Len also built up a wide reputation of his own and started the first medical school in Uganda.

Mengo Hospital, founded in 1897, stands on the slopes of Namirembe hill just below the great cathedral. It is holy ground for the Christian, for in the shadow of that cathedral lie the graves of Mackay, Hannington and Pilkington, pioneers and martyrs of the faith. Below lies the city of Kampala, set in the beauty of its flowering trees, cassias, flame trees, and jacarandas. There was not much of a city in 1914, although the country was beautiful and the climate pleasant, and Dr Cook was a most inspiring leader. The need for medical work was tremendous, and there seemed every reason for the new recruits to settle down and build up the existing work of the hospital and the church.

But both knew this was only the beginning of the journey. This was not the people to whom the Gospel had never been preached. The war dragged on and the bulletins from France became more disastrous and the two active young men must have felt restless indeed in their comparatively safe backwater, but they knew that the backwater was a channel to some unexplored country as yet lost behind the ranges, though just where this country lay they had little idea, until one day in 1916 they happened to start reading a book.

It was a travel book called *In the Heart of Africa*, written by the Duke of Mecklenburg, and it described a mysterious, mythical country of twin kingdoms south of the Uganda border mountains, at that time hardly on the map as far as

civilization was concerned. Its name was Ruanda-Urundi* and
it was no bigger than Ireland. It was the north-west part of
German East Africa and Belgian soldiers sometimes talked of
it, for their troops had had to march through it to their cost.
It was thickly populated, a land of tremendous volcanic mountains, intersected by rivers, with lakes and waterfalls. The high
forest belts sheltered lions, leopards and gorillas and the ruling
tribe was tall and kingly. The two young men read and re-read
the book and their hearts beat faster. This was no ordinary
travel book. God was speaking to them through it and they
must at least go forward and spy out the land.

They were not without encouragement. J. J. Willis, Bishop
of Uganda, believed in their call and aided and abetted them all
the way along. The allied forces were driving the Germans out
of East Africa and the lovely, unknown little country began
to be in the news. In December 1916 the two friends were due
for three weeks' leave and they applied for permission to visit
Rwanda. By some divinely guided accident they were given a
permit, although it transpired later that it had been issued
without the knowledge or consent of the Belgian Government and should never have been given at all. But that discovery came too late; Len and Algie were already far over the
border.

The Rev H. B. Lewin—a C.M.S. missionary in Uganda—
went with them and they travelled on motor-bikes from Kampala to the borders of Uganda, first through the plains where
the long-horned cattle graze and then over the rounded hills
of Kigezi. It was the late rainy season. The roads had been
appalling and they had been soaked to the skin and plastered
in mud. They had left their motor-bikes at the last rest house
and had marched for three days through almost uninhabited
game country, but their weariness was forgotten when they

* The name was spelt thus until 1962, when the two countries became independent and are now known as Rwanda and Burundi. "Ruanda" is still used by
the Mission for its name and as a general term to include the whole area in
which it operates.

climbed the last steep escarpment and looked over for the first time into Rwanda.

It was a bright December evening and their land of promise lay below them, clear shining after rain, green as the Garden of Eden. To the south rose the hills of Rwanda, bathed in that particular moment of cool radiance that precedes the swift equatorial twilight, and the drifts of smoke from myriad huts and banana plantations soften and obscure the deep clefts of the valleys between. Both were seized with an unmistakable conviction that this was their land, "A land of hills and valleys, a land for which the Lord thy God careth from the beginning of the year even unto the end of the year . . . The place that the Lord thy God shall choose, to cause His name to dwell there."

They toured northern Rwanda for nearly three weeks, becoming more entranced each day. They discovered a country that lies on the upland of the chain of mountains and ridges which form the backbone of Africa and the watershed of the Congo and the Nile. To the north-west stand the Bufumbira mountains. These volcanoes, eight in number, stand out like sentinels against the sky on a clear evening, towering above the general level of the Rwanda plateau. Most of them are extinct, but two still open a vent down to the mysterious fires which redden the night sky with their light. On the west is the great rift valley, dividing Rwanda and Burundi from the Congo, and here lies the amazing, geological phenomenon, Lake Tanganyika, four hundred and twenty miles long, hardly more than thirty miles wide, the second deepest freshwater lake in the world; a crack in the earth's surface four thousand seven hundred feet deep. East, the plateau falls away to the dry, scrubby vastness of Tanzania. It was from this side that the doctors, with Mr Lewin as their guide, entered the country on their first safari.

The beginning of 1917 found the doctors back at work in Mengo, but they were men with a new purpose. It was no

longer a matter of finding out the will of God, or seeking for
direction; it was now merely a question of waiting to go forward, and preparing themselves in every way possible for their
life-work. It was not easy to be patient as the months dragged
on, but 1919 came round at last, and with the blessing and
approval of the mission in Uganda, the two young men travelled
back to England with the formidable task ahead of them of
persuading the harassed, war-weary, financially strained C.M.S.
to break out on a new pioneer enterprise to be launched by two
enthusiastic missionaries in their twenties.

Reason, maturity and prudence would have swept the whole
suggestion aside as crazy, especially as both Algie and Len
had lost no time in acquiring wives who would also need sup-
porting. Algie had gone joyfully back to Zoë and they were
married almost immediately. Len married Esther Macdonald,
a buxom, live-wire of a girl, whose practical common sense and
strength of character well fitted her for a pioneer existence.

But the Rev G. T. Manley, Africa Secretary of C.M.S., was
a man of faith, and as deep calls to deep, so he recognized the
call of God in the apparently absurd, untimely proposition. It
was not altogether easy to make his committee recognize it
(especially as there was a baby on the way for Algie and Zoë
by now) and yet the impossible happened and in June 1920 an
article appeared in *The Gleaner* written by Len Sharp, from
which the following is an extract: "Subject to the consent of
the Belgian authorities, the C.M.S. has decided to start missionary work in Rwanda later this year. The decision to open
new work and accept new responsibility at this time of financial
crisis is a courageous step on the part of the C.M.S. committee,
so we offered to be responsible for raising the money for the
first four years. We believe that God will honour this venture
of faith. Dr and Mrs Stanley Smith, my wife and I, hope to
start for Rwanda early this autumn to open a mission hospital
near Nyanza, the king's capital; to be followed, we hope, by a
school for the sons of chiefs." The article was followed by a

statement from the C.M.S.: "The article on Rwanda is worthy of special note for it tells the story of a venture of faith. The debate in the Committee will long be remembered. The financial outlook of the Society was at its blackest and the mandate for Rwanda had just been given to Belgium. These facts seem irresistible and yet the Committee, all but unanimously, decided to advance. What is the meaning of this? Other factors there may have been, but the one which weighed most heavily was the feeling that the strong sense of compulsion in the two doctors *was* the call of God, alike to them and the Society."

Thrilling weeks followed as the young couples prepared to sail and proved again and again that God was going to provide for them sometimes through most unexpected channels. For instance, they had never met the army officer whose car, while he was driving through Tunbridge Wells one Sunday morning, suddenly developed engine trouble and had to be left in a garage. To pass the time, he went into the church where Canon Stather Hunt was telling about the new Ruanda venture. Touched by what he heard, the officer gave £500 towards it as a thankoffering for God's mercy to him in the war.

The next move was to obtain the sanction of Belgium, which now administered Rwanda. Through the help of Monsieur Anet, of the Belgian Protestant Church, who had been asked by the government to organize the taking over of the old German mission stations, the doctors were taken to see the Minister of Colonies and permission was given to them to reside in Burundi in the south. The doors were open—the way was clear; and in November 1920 the four set out with baby Nora Stanley Smith, only a few months old. Their hopes were high and their hearts full of praise and courage.

They had got as far as Marseille when a letter reached them from the Belgian Government saying that permission to enter Ruanda-Urundi had been withdrawn. The door was closed after all. One might say, slammed in their faces. Yet all four agreed that they must not go back. They would go on to Uganda and await further developments. So they set sail through the Mediterranean, "under sealed orders known only to our Guide."

2

Foundations

The journey from the coast to Uganda was blazing hot, and a rather limp little party arrived in Kampala to find themselves the object of fierce discussion. Some wished to send them to Kenya; others to Teso in the north-east to support flourishing existing work, but Higher Authority had told them to turn south. The door of their promised land might, as yet, be closed, but at least they must be ready and at hand for the day when the doors would open, and Bishop Willis again supported them against those who thought otherwise, assigning them to Kabale in the southern Kigezi district, a wild, mountainous region at the foot of the Bufumbira range. It was near the borders of Rwanda and some of the Rwanda people had come over into British territory, so there was every hope of making a start on the language. An Indian assistant surgeon was running a primitive government dispensary there, and a number of African Christian volunteers went with them. The population at that time was about 200,000 lawless tribes-people.

It was obviously no place for an English baby, so Algie took his reluctant wife to stay with missionaries at Mbarara and Len and Esther Sharp, accompanied by a puppy, started out on the two hundred and sixty miles journey on a motor-bike in February 1921, and a string of porters followed behind with the luggage piled high on their heads. Esther wore skirts to her ankles, which trailed in the rich, red earth of Ankole, and the spluttering machine attracted crowds all the way along. There were no roads, only tracks over the steamy plains, until the rolling country began to rise and they saw ahead of them bare, rounded hills; and then even the tracks stopped. They were confronted by a green mountain, and there was nothing to be done but to leave the motor-bike at the bottom (it was retrieved later with ropes) and climb it—Len on his feet, Esther on her hands and knees, and the puppy on its four paws. Somehow they reached the top and then Len, at least, probably forgot his weariness.

The whole fair district of Kigezi was around them. The rains were over but the great panorama of hills was richly green and fertile, and the valleys were thickly populated; uncountable little huts amidst the plantations, thousands of people who had never known the light of the Gospel. Only a few more miles now, and their life-work would begin.

On 24th February they pitched their tent on the bare, windy summit called Kabira, a mile from the government post of Kabale, and consternation spread amongst the local population. One old man, later baptized as Benjamin, was hoeing when the extraordinary cavalcade approached, with those two fearful pale-faces amongst them. Crowds gathered around the tent and their alarm increased when, three days later, Algie and Bishop Willis arrived on donkeys and started measuring out the building site. Their team of Christian volunteers came with them, and then things really began to hum as the two young doctors started building. Mud and wattle huts began to go up; timber was brought from twelve miles away to build a hospital. The tiny handfuls of local Christians (the result of H. B. Lewin's work in Ankole) rejoiced when they realized what was happening, and proved valuable helpers.

What were their first impressions? For the two young doctors, an overwhelming sense of need and opportunity. The people of the district were noted for drunkenness and witchcraft and on safari it was not unusual to enter villages and find all the children, as well as the adults, sprawled on the earth in a drunken stupor. Nobody appeared to want them or trust them at first, which left them the freer to build. They had no money to employ skilled labour so they themselves had to teach the local Africans, and their workmen became their first mission field. Daily they preached to them and one day, after a talk on the love of God, a hush seemed to fall on the squatting crowd. They went off to their homes saying, "Praise God! Praise God!" and from then onwards one or another would ask the doctor to visit his home. A few started to read and immediately became teachers of others. Hostility gave way to respect, and respect to confidence. They discovered that the white man's medicines were neither bitter nor harmful, and morning by morning figures would creep through the mist and huddle on the verandah; a terrible collection of jiggers (parasites which bury themselves in the flesh), dysentery, ulcers, yaws, leprosy, tuberculosis—filthy and hopeless. It was not always possible to treat them without a proper hospital, but the doctors did their best. That strangulated hernia, for instance! There was neither anaesthetic nor operating theatre, so the Indian assistant held the conscious patient down on a bed of banana leaves, the doctor operated and the man recovered to live a long, active life.

Seeds sprang to saplings in the prolific tropical climate, and walls mounted and the bright air re-echoed with the stroke of axe and hammer and mallet. And yet, there was no sense of permanence in the hearts of the two young men. This, they knew, was only the first step of the journey for only twenty miles away, between a gap in the hills, Mt Muhabura reared its conical head, one of the volcanoes right on the border of Rwanda. Climb to the hilly top of a ridge and you could see a tree that marked the boundary. Nobody knows how many times a day, in their imagination and prayers they travelled across that boundary.

They were hard, thrilling days for the young men, but perhaps not quite so thrilling for the young bride, who was starting her first pregnancy in such primitive conditions. Besides, apart from the hardships and the loneliness of having no other white woman to speak to, she was frightened of these primitive people. "I was very afraid of the wild Bakiga," she wrote later. "They wore very inadequate skins and tore about and shouted in an unknown tongue, and I did wish they wouldn't!" Nevertheless, she made a real home of the mud hut and planted a garden that soon made the hill a blaze of beauty; wattles, eucalyptus, cassias and jacarandas grew quickly and in May, Constance Watney arrived to work as matron in the makeshift hospital, so there was someone else to talk to. And just a month later, a suitable house having been built, Zoë arrived with Nora, and the people came from far and wide to see a white baby and touch her flaxen hair. Together the young wives gathered the children and taught them by tracing letters on the sand. More and more arrived, and the need for a school-teacher became a priority in their planning and praying.

Housekeeping was a problem. All stores had to be carried two hundred and sixty miles on the heads of porters from Kampala, and what one needed did not exactly arrive overnight. Later on the group acquired a cart, which cut down shopping expeditions to three months there and back, but even this had its disadvantages for they were at the mercy of their packers and if the kerosene overflowed into the sack of flour, there was nothing to be done but to put up with the unusual flavour until next time. Also, some articles deteriorated *en route*. The Sharps' sofa was used as a bed by the carter every night of the journey from Kampala, and arrived so infested with bugs that it could not be allowed in the house.

In 1923 Constance Hornby arrived to start a girls' school. She had already worked for some years in other parts of Uganda but she was a born pioneer and the Kigezi district is still her home. (She lives on at Kabale, loved and honoured by generations of women.) She started her school with eleven little urchins clad in skins and dirt, scratching their letters in the sand, and to them she gave all her life and love. Supported by the Girls' Friendly Society in England, she wrote long, vivid letters describing the joys and sorrows of those early days. At first it was hard to persuade pupils to come, but she would travel any distance to gain a child. She would tramp miles and miles over hills and valleys, through elephant-infested country with African porters and a group of her dear girls. One glad day she persuaded some chiefs to give her six of their daughters to train and educate. The children were most unwilling, but were forced to follow her and that night they camped and lay down to sleep. Only in the morning did Miss Hornby discover that all six had run away. Nothing daunted, she went back over two mountains and found them sitting within sight of their homes, weeping bitterly. There was much talking and arguing and then the chiefs, unwilling to be defied by their daughters, sent the mothers to escort them to their journey's end, and so they travelled back to Kabale, like Jeremiah's company, with weeping and wailing and supplications. But Miss Hornby won the battle. The wailing mothers went back to the village, and the weeping children remained with her and became bright, happy schoolgirls.

A rebel by nature, she waged war on tyranny, dirt, the oppression and slavery of women, and child marriages. How indignant she became when, on asking a man why none of the girls in his district came to school, he replied, "Would you teach a cow to read or send a cow to church?" But she didn't always get the better of the Africans, as the following extract from a letter shows:

"I believe this is the most unwashed, undressed part of the world. I was talking to the chief and teacher about things and they had to agree that people could wash, but what about the dressing part? 'Well,' they said, 'what would you do?' 'Oh,' I said, 'I'd buy a baby goat for 6d.' (Roars of laughter.) 'But where would you get 6d. from? And it would have to grow up and it would be sure to die.' So that was no good. 'Oh, well, I would dig and get food and sell it.' 'But who would buy your food? Everyone digs and grows their own!' So I had to give in."

The school grew and grew for there were many attractions. "I don't mind if she becomes a Christian or not. I want her to be clean," said one father. She found it almost impossible to turn any needy child away. "Agnesi came to me on safari, very dirty in a wee goat skin and with a water pot. 'I have come to be your child,' she said, but of course this could not be. I went to find her people—and what a home! The father, an invalid sitting outside a dirty grass hut, absolutely refused and I came away sad. However, three weeks later she arrived with a porter, and now she is my child."

"Another day a widow woman died, leaving a small girl of about four or five. The chief asked me to have pity on her, and, my word, she was an object of pity! Just a little bag of bones! So I said that they could send her along when she was out of quarantine and the other day she arrived, footsore and un- clad, her only possession in the world a stick that had belonged to her brother, which he had given her to walk with. She would not be parted from this. It was dinner time, so I got a girl to carry her down for food, but she crept back to fetch the stick, and later on I told the children to bring her in to school and again she brought the stick and sat hugging it. But in the evening Nora Stanley Smith brought her a doll and a dress, and at last she went to bed with the doll in her arms. Kaburahona is her name and she is the sort of little person you feel you must be very gentle and tender with. So that is the way we reduce our school to reasonable dimensions."

Overworked, overcrowded, often living from hand to mouth, Miss Hornby learned along with her children, rejoicing in their pranks and progress. Once, walking through a deep valley, she and her girls were in real danger from a herd of wild elephants which charged across the road. The wind was blowing away from them, and they crouched, praying. As the herd crashed away in the trees, they drew a sigh of relief and prepared to run, but one child stopped them. "Wait! Wait!" she cried. "We haven't said 'Thank you'."

"What do you want to say 'sorry' for tonight?" she asked a group of her smallest.

"Envy," replied one promptly. "I envy you every time I see the sheets on your bed." So she tried to live even more simply, although at the best of times it was a primitive existence. She wrote to her Girls' Friendly Society pleading unashamedly for dresses, soap, material, dolls, pencils and notebooks, and they responded magnificently, but there were still times when it was impossible to make ends meet. At the end of one month she called her young teacher and told her sadly that she could not give her her monthly salary of three shillings. The girl smiled, unconcerned. "I do not need it," she replied, "I have all." And at the end of the second month she was still quite unconcerned.

But at the end of the third month Miss Hornby was really distressed. She believed that God had promised to provide their needs and it seemed as though He had failed them. She shut herself up to pray for this particular need, and sure enough, a letter arrived with a ten-shilling note. How joyfully she handed over the three months' pay; the girl rejoiced, too, and their faith was strengthened. Only when Miss Hornby went to bed that night did she find the money returned by her bedside. "What do I need with money?" the young teacher repeated. "Have not I got all?"

So the girls grew up on simple New Testament lines of faith and self-denial. A spirit of covetousness had not yet crept in, and those first young teachers were content to work simply for God and their children. They gathered round their leader and learned from her life and example. She prayed earnestly for a helper but none had come when her first furlough was due, and she could not give her children back to the evil, filth and squalor of their heathen homes. Shelter was offered for some of them at the Mbarara school in Uganda, so she and fifteen of her pupils set out on foot, luggage on their heads, to cross the steep Kigezi mountains and the hot Ankole plains. Day after day they marched on, camping at night. Twelve weary children were received at Mbarara; three tramped on with Miss Hornby towards Kampala. Altogether they covered two hundred and forty-five miles on foot before Mrs Cook picked them up in a car and took charge of the three. Then, with every child safe and cared for, Miss Hornby left for England. On her return journey she hired a lorry, and she and her children came back singing and praising God, to Kabale.

But all this, and much more, was going on against the background of personal sorrow and sickness. Constance Watney was invalided home after a year's devoted nursing in unbelievably primitive conditions, and Beatrix Martin had come to take her place. The story goes that she was nearly turned back from a life of useful missionary service by the sight of Lutobo hill, up which she was being escorted by Miss Hornby. Tired out by the climb, she stopped dead half-way up the muddy slope. "I can't go on," she said. "You'll have to," said Miss Hornby, "you can't stay here." So she crawled over the summit and arrived at Kabale, twenty miles farther on, faint, yet pursuing.

Esther Sharp had had her first baby and had also taken on the care of the District Commissioner's baby, as his wife had died of septicaemia shortly after her confinement. Esther guarded these babies scrupulously, almost fanatically, while dysentery, leprosy, septicaemia, tuberculosis and typhus raged around them. Little Robin Sharp lived to be eight months old and the light of his mother's eyes in that hard, lonely battlefield. Then God took him. Dr Sharp himself was stricken with dysentery and Esther became ill with grieving and anxiety. Zoë tried hard to help and care for her, but the sight of the two Stanley Smith babies only emphasized her loss. The work was leaping ahead as fast as the trees were sprouting on the formerly bare Kabira hill, but the five workers were almost spent. In 1924 Len Sharp decided to go home and look for reinforcements.

Just before he left, his hospital was finished and officially opened by Sir Geoffrey Archer, the Governor of Uganda. It was a building of unusual design; five blocks connected by covered corridors, built in sun-dried brick with a papyrus roof. It was an impressive ceremony. A large contingent of leading Europeans arrived and the five big chiefs of the Kigezi counties sat facing the Governor. The hospital, with its one hundred and twenty-five beds, was dedicated to the glory of God and the service of suffering humanity. It was a beautiful, fitting tribute to all that had been achieved, but perhaps the most telling memorial of the love and struggle and sacrifices of those early years is the tiny white cross under the eucalyptus trees with its simple inscription, "Robin Leonard Sharp, infant son of Leonard and Esther. With Christ."

3

Reinforcements

"Such rapidity of progress carried with it the seeds of danger. Where European and national staff alike are relatively young and inexperienced; where converts are so quickly made before qualified leaders can be trained, the danger of a landslide cannot be forgotten, but we may thank God for the work done and believe 'that He which has begun a good work will perform it until the day of Jesus Christ'." So wrote Bishop Willis.

Dr Sharp, looking back on those early years of the Ruanda Mission, outlined its aims in the following words:

"There are three main needs requiring to be met in every mission field.

"First, a growing band of home friends and supporters whose organized effort, prayers and gifts make advance possible.

"Secondly, an adequate number of new missionaries coming out to seize and use every fresh opportunity that arises in evangelistic, medical, teaching and translational spheres of work.

"Thirdly, the blessing of God, seen not merely in numerous native adherents, nor even in an apparently prosperous, well-organized native church, but through these happy signs of missionary success, the calling out of a living Church; men, women, children, who have come to know the Lord Jesus Christ as their own Saviour from the guilt and stain of past sin and from its power day by day. Men and women growing in grace, fruitful in service, and in likeness to Christ."

It was not only for the sake of Esther's health and his own

35

that Dr Sharp decided to take a furlough as early as 1924. Three years before, he and Dr Stanley Smith had started a work that had grown to an alarming magnitude. There was every "happy sign of missionary success", but there were also causes for real alarm, as those vivid quotations, for all their outmoded terminology, make clear.

On the financial side things were not very business-like. The original thirty or so 'Friends of Ruanda' were almost a family affair led by Mrs Sharp and Mrs Macdonald, the mothers of Len and Esther, with Norman Sharp responsible for the accounts. But the support of buildings, new mission stations, schools, hospitals and new missionaries was far beyond the means of this loving, faithful little band. The need and scope of the Ruanda Mission required to be far more widely known.

Also, there could be no further real advance without new European missionaries, for the more widely they sowed, the more impossible it became to plough deeply. And they had sown very widely indeed. Dr Stanley Smith had travelled west as far as the Congo borders, establishing small churches, leaving teachers and catechists, and Dr Sharp had explored one hundred and fifty miles to the south. Teachers from Uganda had answered the appeal and nobly come to their rescue, but they were sorely tried by the hardships and loneliness and they themselves badly needed teaching and help, as this rather pathetic letter from one of these teachers shows:

"These are the things I have seen here: hills, and nothing but hills stretching everywhere; bitter cold exceeding that of Uganda; the food consisting of two kinds of flour, peas, beans and a few potatoes, but this food gives us no joy. However, we look not at the earthly joy for ours is a heavenly joy in Christ Jesus. Pray that my wife and myself may be enabled to do all to which we are called; that the very steep hills may not be too much for us; nor the cold, nor the unaccustomed food overcome us.

"Yet people are anxious to read and everyone who is baptized wants to go and teach others. And here is proof that they are anxious to read. Every day, many come beseeching teachers to go and teach them, and others come to work to obtain shillings to buy drums as they want two drums in every church. And every day girls come from heathen fathers, who want them to marry Christian husbands, and many put cents in the bag. My friends, these things show how eager the people of this country are to learn of God."

And to the more discerning they also show just what Christianity meant to these faithful, sincere, devoted young teachers. Literacy, a church with drums, marriage between those who had learnt their creed and catechism, and cents in the bag. Truly there were "numerous adherents", but few real, transforming conversions. Small wonder that Dr Stanley Smith wrote in 1922, "A safari around the village churches always sends one to one's knees in prayer for a revival of spiritual religion. But if our teachers are to be revived, we who lead them must be abiding in the place of power." But with all the will in the world two could not teach and shepherd such a widely scattered flock, and attend to the rapidly growing medical and pastoral work at Kabale. Surely, surely, faced by such unparalleled opportunity some would hear the word of God and come.

Dr Sharp, in his time, has been used by God to call many out to the mission field, and as a result of his first furlough five joined the ranks, each trained and prepared in a marvellous way to man the strategic posts: Captain Holmes the pioneer; Jack Warren the teacher and pastor; Miss Davis the nurse; the Rev H. E. Guillebaud the translator—and his wife.

Captain Geoffrey Holmes was an officer and the captain of the British army ice hockey team, and he gave up a promising army and sporting career in order to join the Mission. Miss Davis later joined Miss Martin at Kabale hospital and worked valiantly for five years.

The Rev Jack Warren! Forty-six years later, wrinkled faces

in Kigezi still light up at the name. Brought up in a C.M.S. missionary home, he had helped to found the Inter-Varsity Fellowship and had worked widely for the Children's Special Service Mission. A patch on his lung, which developed during the war, had forced him to rest but rest never came easily to him. He had always wanted to be a missionary overseas and Dr Sharp spoke of a country where the high mountain air might even help his complaint. He offered himself at once, and was out at Kabale before the end of the year.

He came like a tonic to the tired little company, with a zeal and energy that far outdid his actual physical strength and there was no repressing him. Children flocked to him wherever he went, and he came with the love and gifts and prayers of many little English children behind him. Even his journey was fraught with excitement. He did conjuring tricks on the boat to crowds of exuberant little Belgian boys and girls, and preached to them in his "extra special best French". At Kampala he assembled and mounted his new motor-bike, which had travelled out with him, and offered to take Geoffrey Holmes pillion to Kabale, but it was the rainy season and the roads were slippery and muddy. They capsized and Geoffrey Holmes's shoulder was broken and the motor-bike was smashed up.

He arrived eventually, nothing daunted, to find a little grass shanty church and a handful of poorly trained teachers. With clear-sighted vision he drew up a policy for a future he would never see. There must be a boys' school to train evangelists and teachers from childhood, and to send out grounded men of God into the districts. And there must be a solid, beautiful church where little scattered congregations could gather for united fellowship and teaching. He then plunged into the work with such joyful intensity that he had a lung haemorrhage within the first few months and was ordered to rest. But prayer was made for him and he recovered, and the best medical advice in the country bade him carry on.

The boys' school started almost immediately and Dr Stanley Smith remembers with a chuckle, "Some celebration when a crowd of little boys in red fez caps and English costume all arrived to present a goat!" Jack Warren taught them tirelessly, prepared them for baptism and confirmation, played football, jumped and swam with them, which latter he had no business to do; and in three years he laid the foundations of many a young life. "In him I first saw what the love of God was like," said one of his boys later on.

The task he faced in the leadership of the church was a superhuman one. On top of his language study, he was appointed supervisor of an evangelistic work going on in one hundred and fifty village churches, over an area seventy-five miles long by forty-five wide, and the building of a great central church at Kabale itself. Many of the children in England, who loved him, sent money for that church and in November 1925 the foundation-stone was laid higher up the hill above the hospital. Eleven months later, on 13th October 1926, the tower was fixed in position amidst great rejoicings. Lindesay Guillebaud, then nine years old, has described that never-to-be-forgotten event.

"The erection of the steeple, so huge on the ground, so small in position, was a major operation with, of course, no cranes or mechanical help. I remember Dr Sharp in control of a big team of African helpers with scaffolding and ladders and ropes, and the thrill with which we watched the steeple, teetering to one side or the other as directions were shouted by Dr Sharp, balanced on the slippery roof. But it finally came to rest in position and all the Africans gave a mighty yell of triumph."

The Africans themselves were thrilled with their new church and gave generously towards the cost of the building. At the Christmas services a collection was taken in every church in Kigezi, where some gave a cent and some brought cows, and goats and chickens. There was real sacrificial giving, too, like

39

that of the gardener who returned nearly half his monthly wage. On 16th June 1927, the church was consecrated by Bishop Willis and Jack Warren's cup overflowed. "I will try and describe this glorious day," he wrote. "At 10 a.m. on June the sixteenth, with church and both vestries crowded with close on two thousand people and hundreds outside, the Bishop knocked on the South door. It was opened and the service of consecration began. Our debt that morning stood at £35. To our great joy this was more than met. Nine bulls and cows, thirty-three sheep and goats, over a thousand chickens and twelve hundred and fifty eggs, as well as £10 in the collection, provided over £50. This wonderful array of gifts in kind was parked outside on the lawn and, fortunately, the glass in the windows somewhat muted the lowing of oxen, the bleating of sheep and the cackling of the fowl."

They were happy years of achievement for Jack Warren, for he was by nature a happy man who loved life and all its good gifts, and to some it seemed as though he sought to crowd all that life could hold of love and laughter into the brief span allotted to him.

"On the eleventh 'weekaversary' of the laying of the first brick of my very own little home," he wrote, "I moved into it, and there certainly is no place like home, and I am delighted beyond words to be in my own at last. My garden was made before the house, and is looking lovely with roses, carnations, violets, antirrhinums, dahlias and chrysanthemums, and other varieties all going strong." In 1927 he married Dr Kathleen Ardill, their wedding being the first service to be held in his own church and it went off, as might be expected, in hilarious style. A year later their baby, Sheelagh, was born and his joy was complete.

But below the exuberant surface there was deep suffering and agony. He had no illusions about the spiritual quality of some of the evangelists and teachers of his vast district. As early as 1926 he wrote an appeal to friends at home. "Again and again we get terrible setbacks to the work by the failure of some of our teachers . . . so we beseech you to agonize in prayer for us. Pray until it hurts, that the mighty indwelling, keeping power of the Holy Spirit may be experienced by the Christians. One sees, sometimes, just the faintest signs of working in their hearts, but more often no sign at all, and without that power no young teacher can run straight amidst the terrible temptations to which they are exposed. Think of these boys with no sermon to help them; no books to read, just a Bible or Testament of which they know but a small part and only read laboriously; surrounded by heathenism and spirit worship and with practically no Christian fellowship, and then you won't blame them when they fall, but praise God that any ever stand at all."

In February 1927 he asked for a special week of prayer. "There are now close on two thousand baptized Christians, but we are only too conscious that the signs of real heart change are very few and far between. Moral lapse upon lapse, and tragedy upon tragedy, have been following one on top of the other. Only this week comes the evidence that one of our most trusted teachers has been stealing the church members' money. Two old men, learning the catchism, thanked me so pitifully when I returned their money. Another senior teacher has been drinking heavily and has been dismissed. We plead with every Friend of Ruanda to set aside a time on each of the above ten days to wrestle in prayer with us, and then we know that we may indeed expect a wonderful outpouring of the Holy Spirit, not limited to Kigezi, but a flood that will reach the uttermost parts of Rwanda in days to come."

Jack Warren did not live to see the answer to his prayer, or to witness the flood flowing beyond Rwanda to the uttermost part of the earth. He was taken very ill in the spring of 1928 and it was clear that his work in Africa must be laid down. On Easter Sunday, just before leaving, he gave his last message to a packed congregation, "Whosoever believeth on Me shall never die." It was a comfort to him to leave the work he had built up in the hands of a promising new recruit, Lawrence Barham. His last months of sickness were gallantly, merrily borne and he died in England on 20th January 1929.

While the Church grew the medical work at Kabale had also been growing apace. The hospital, which held a hundred and twenty-five beds, flourished under the able leadership of Dr Sharp. The sick came from far and wide but it, too, had its quota of discouragement and opposition, as trained senior workers had to be expelled for immorality and drinking.

In November 1925 a visit from Bishop Willis was expected, but during the afternoon a tremendous thunderstorm broke out and the end block of the new hospital was struck by lightning. The thatch went up in a blaze in spite of torrential rain, and while those on the spot carried out the patients (fifty sick men from the first block) it must have seemed that the whole hospital was doomed.

But they had reckoned without its architect. Dr Sharp should have been away meeting the Bishop, but his car was out of action so, in God's mercy, he was still on the spot.

"The tall, lean, tanned figure striding up the path meant that whatever had gone wrong was about to be put right," wrote one who was a child at the time, and no doubt on this occasion Dr Sharp sprinted up the path. He attacked the first corridor, but soon realized that they could not save the second block, containing the most seriously ill and the dying. He ordered them all to be carried out at top speed while he himself, with superhuman strength, uprooted the posts that supported the third corridor and started to tear down the thatch with his bare hands. It was difficult to get intelligent assistance owing to the frenzied excitement, and tools were locked up and could not be procured in time; but the break was made in the building and the third block, where all the valuable hospital apparatus was housed, was saved.

The Bishop arrived to find a scene of wild confusion: two-fifths of the hospital in smoking ruins, the remaining wards overflowing and the women's ward, designed for eighteen, holding seventy. He also found a company of somewhat scorched and blackened missionaries who were, however, praising God for the miracle of what had been preserved. No lives had been lost and no one had been seriously hurt. The confirmation service went through as planned, on the damp, muddy hillside in sight of the wreckage.

But, as so often happened, the disaster proved a blessing. At the service next day, staff and patients, pastors and congregation prayed that the money would be sent to rebuild, and the response from the faithful Friends of Ruanda and the Church in Uganda was immediate. Within seven months or so the wards were in use again, the dangerous thatch had been replaced by galvanized iron roofs, and the floors had been cemented. Dr Sharp wrote, "It will indeed be a great relief when so much time need not be spent on supervising building. In six months time buildings for each department of the work at Kabale will be finished. These buildings may be only brick and mortar, but it is a privilege to build them for God, for they alone make possible all the labour of love and the work of the Spirit which they enshrine."

For there was a work of the Spirit going on. As tiny new shoots in spring are hidden under the weight of dead leaves, and germinating seeds lie deep in the cold earth, so, almost unrecognized under the mass of ignorance, nominal religion and hypocrisy, there were everywhere the small stirrings and whispers of new life. For instance, in 1922 a poor, dirty lad covered with sores was admitted to the men's ward; and his name was Yosiya Kinuka, who was destined to become one of God's leaders in the land.

4

The Translation

A year after the arrival of the Sharps and Stanley Smiths at Kabale, thrilling news reached them. The Belgian Government had agreed to transfer a wide strip of Eastern Rwanda, about a hundred miles long, to Britain for the purpose of surveying a route for a Cape to Cairo railway.

Were these fast-closed doors about to open? It seemed so. Dr Sharp lost no time in writing to ask permission to start work, and received a most cordial reply from the British Provincial Commissioner, suggesting that the young doctors meet the District Commissioner at the border to discuss plans and promising them every assistance.

It was a great day when they set out together along the valley to climb the ridge at which they had so often gazed. As, at last, they looked over the rolling, thickly populated highlands of Rwanda, they felt like Caleb and Joshua. Six years ago they had spied out the land, now surely the time had come to go and conquer it for an inheritance. There between earth and sky, they prayed that they might possess it for Christ, and rededicated themselves to God for the task.

With quickened hope and faith they went on to meet the District Commissioner. He turned out to be a man Dr Sharp had known in the war, and a Christian. He offered them complete freedom to travel round and to choose any site they pleased for what in those days was called a mission station. Dr Sharp went straight over the border and explored for three weeks, and everywhere he went he found that the place had been prepared. While they had waited for those doors to open, hundreds had been praying, and now men were ready and eager and willing to hear the Gospel. The tall, athletic Batutsi chiefs were particularly friendly and wherever he went crowds gathered for medical treatment and the people asked for teachers. Great was his joy when one night, his work finished at last, a chief, six-foot-five tall, drew him aside. "I want to be taught the words of Jesus," he said, "but it must be a secret, no one must know."

It was a glorious homecoming, to tell the rest of the little group what he had found, and to write back to the Friends of Ruanda, "Let us go up at once and possess the land, for we are well able to overcome it." But this meant additional man-power, African evangelists and reinforcements from England. No one could be spared from Kabale and the missionaries were not yet forthcoming, but again the Church of Uganda re-sponded.

During the war years Dr Sharp had been sent by the Govern-ment to Toro hospital in western Uganda and the church there remembered him well. When the urgent appeal for African evangelists went forth, Ezekieri, an outstanding young Christian, came to join his old friend, bringing with him a band of eight young men from different districts of Uganda. They were placed at strategic points along the proposed railway strip and they may be counted among the early heroes of the Mission. Far from their friends in a high, cold, uncivilized country, savage in its customs and speaking a strange language, they hung on, living and preaching Christ and sowing the first seeds of that mighty harvest field.

But even greater than the need for hospitals, preachers or foreign missionaries, was the need of the Word of God in the Rwanda language. The Uganda teachers taught their wild congregations their letters, creed and catechism, but there was no Gospel to put into their hands, no Sword of the Spirit with which to fight their battles and no one as yet to translate it, although a start had been made on the New Testament by the Belgian Protestant Mission. This was a matter that weighed heavily on Dr Sharp's mind when he travelled home in 1924 to seek new recruits.

Jack Warren, Geoffrey Holmes and Miss Davis had already sailed and Dr Sharp was planning to return the following month, but he was ill and, to his great disappointment, his doctor insisted on a further three months' convalescence. It was hard to rest with his mind leaping forwards towards the open door of his land of promise, but had he not stayed he would never have come in contact with the Rev Harold E. Guillebaud.

It seemed like a chance meeting with the tall, delicate man with his deceivingly simple manner and almost childlike sense of humour, who had once backed him on a difficult council meeting when the whole future of the Ruanda Mission was at stake. Harold Guillebaud and his wife had offered to the C.M.S. for missionary work in Uganda, but had been refused on health grounds. A brilliant linguist and scholar, he had settled down with his large family in England, but at the beginning of 1925 Dr Sharp talked to him about the five million people of Rwanda and Burundi and the eight teachers who had no book to give them, and once again Harold and Margaret Guillebaud heard the call that cut across sense and reason. They acted exceedingly quickly. They found a home for Peter, their eldest, and their twins of four, and within a few months they arrived at Kabale with their remaining three little daughters.

Rosemary (10), Lindesay (8), and Philippa (6) travelled from Kampala in Dr Sharp's car and he promptly became their hero. Like their elders, they had to get out at the bottom of Lutobo hill and climb it on small, aching legs, but the view at the top entranced them. They were entering a new, fairy, mist-wreathed country, "beanstalk country", Uncle Len called it, and there were presents waiting for them when they arrived, three soft, purring, grey kittens. Contrary to all popular foreboding, the children settled down at once, loved their new land and grew up to serve it.

Harold Guillebaud settled down at once, too, with a scholarly disregard for his surroundings, while Margaret Guillebaud made the necessary arrangements for her children's safety and education. It was worrying in the mornings to find shrouded figures huddled on their verandah looking larger than life in the thick mists, who often turned out to be leprosy patients mistaking the Guillebaud's house for the hospital. She erected a hedge in order to keep out such unsuitable visitors, but Harold Guillebaud was the most accessible of men and people kept getting through the hedge. Like the rest of the missionary world in their generation, the early Ruanda missionaries were true colonials: loving, selfless, devoted as they were to the Africans, they were a race apart and the local people looked up to them and kept their "proper" places . . . on the verandah. But Harold Guillebaud created a precedent by inviting in, first the houseboy, and then his friends, to his Sunday evening family hymn singing. Some eyebrows were raised, but he was always rather oblivious to raised eyebrows and more and more delighted Rwanda-speaking Africans would crowd in. The Guillebaud children would choose the hymns, their father would explain the meaning to the guests, and often, as the family sang it in English, he would sing it impromptu in the local language. Afterwards he would write it down, Mrs Guillebaud would duplicate it on the Gestetner during the week, and all would learn it the following Sunday. The hymn-book for Rwanda sprang from these happy Sunday evenings and so, perhaps, did the seeds of a new idea that was already beginning to take root in the minds of a few. Was real Christian brotherhood with the Africans really possible and practical? Could Christ break down barriers of race and colour? And was there some common ground where men stood before God as equals? The outworking of the answer lay far in the future, but at least the question had been suggested.

The Translation

Harold Guillebaud started his translation of the Gospel for Rwanda almost as soon as he arrived. He travelled down into Rwanda to discuss the project with Monsieur Honoré, a Belgian missionary who had already started on the work and was glad to hand over the manuscript to a full-time translator. With the help of Samsoni Inyarubuga, a highly intelligent Tutsi of the minority but ruling tribe, he started by the unusual method of learning the language by means of the translation. He wrote of his work as follows:

"As regards my own work, I receive a constant flow of pure Rwanda from Samsoni and I have to find out the meaning of each new word and construction. Samsoni translates, and I make sure that he has got the sense of the original. He knows Runyoro and Ruganda and refers constantly to the Bibles in these languages for which he, in fact, translates. Then I have to find out the meaning of what he said by explanation and gesture and, if he seems off the track, I have to explain the meaning to him. It is fascinating work, especially when one has the thrill of discovering a brand new tense, and as the number of tenses is legion I may have a good many such thrills before I have done. There is plenty of writing to do because every new word must be entered in the dictionary, and every item of information on the grammar and syntax must be written up and card indexed, but it is work after my own heart and I love every minute of it."

Only a year later he writes, "I rejoice to tell you that St Mark's Gospel and the book of prayers and hymns (25 in number) have been sent off to England to be printed and St Matthew's Gospel is nearly finished. The other day when I repeated some of the prayers and hymns a young Tutsi said, 'It is good Kinyarwanda such as we speak.' "

He was infinitely patient and careful. Criticisms about spelling made him revise and re-copy the whole Gospel, but the work gripped him and at the beginning of 1927 he realized that the three years' service he had promised the Mission was only the beginning. "God has been giving us a clear call that He wants us, not for short service, but for life-work." He went home to make permanent arrangements, leaving the following triumphant record of under two years' achievement.

"St Mark's Gospel has been translated, printed and sent out.

"The other three Gospels and the Epistles of St John have been translated and will be revised in collaboration with Monsieur Honoré.

"The baptism service, marriage and burial services, together with the communion service, have been translated and are being printed locally."

The translating involved a lot more than sitting at a desk. Monsieur Honoré, the Belgian missionary who revised the whole of the New Testament, lived in a back-of-beyond district of Rwanda called Remera, whither Harold Guillebaud travelled two or three times a year with his wife and daughters. A car had never been seen there before, and the people were wildly excited. "It is a house that runs," they cried, and his was the first British car and British driver to go right through to the centre of Rwanda.

Mrs Guillebaud was his driver and she wrote a vivid account of what these translation expeditions really meant. "We have actually come here in a car, a thing that has never been done before. The really exciting part of the drive was from Kigali, and Monsieur Honoré very kindly came to meet us and show us the way. First of all we had to cross the river and this was no easy matter. The ferry pontoon is made of two canoes lashed together with a few boards across, and there is considerable danger that in driving one's car on, one will go off into the water on the other side. Then, too, one must get sufficiently into the middle of the raft not to overbalance. The raft is pulled hand over hand across the river, very hard work for the current is frightfully swift and the river teems with crocodiles. The opposite shore is a sandbank and the only way of getting off is to have the car dragged up by ropes. Altogether it is a hair-raising job, but the really thrilling part is seven miles from Remera, where there is no road, only a native path. Monsieur Honoré assured me he had measured it all the way to see it would be wide enough, but it was really laughable to think of getting a car along. One started by turning suddenly off the road over a steep bank and along a hillside very much on the slant, then one descended into a narrow valley and crossed the stream and up a rocky path; and the car sort of clung like a fly to the hillside and one hoped she would not turn over."

To crown it all, that first year there was famine in Remera, and as they worked they were surrounded by starving crowds who thronged the mission for what relief Monsieur Honoré was able to give. On another visit Lindesay was bitten by a dog, and out there in the wilds, miles from proper medical help, her leg became gangrenous. But a nurse was available, the little group prayed, the child was healed and the translation went on.

In spite of the setbacks, journeys and difficulties, the day came when he was able to write, "February the 13th, 1930 is the date that will always live in my memory for the happy moment when I called my wife and Rosemary into my study to hear the last few verses translated. Now there is the revision to be done."

Family problems loomed large. The children's governess was about to get married. Their permanent support was not assured. It seemed that they would have to go home; a prospect that he, at least, found hard to face. "We have not given up hope", he wrote, "that we should complete our four years ending in spring 1932, but will you pray that, if it be His will, we may be able to remain. I had hoped to translate the Psalms, the grammar and a dictionary and though, of course, it is purely a personal matter, I think you will all understand how I yearn to have the joy of seeing with my own eyes the Rwanda New Testament in the hands of the people." And God opened the way. Harold Guillebaud was there on 27th November 1931, when the parcels arrived and he took them down, in person, to Rwanda.

He went home in 1932, leaving behind him in print for Rwanda, the New Testament, prayers and hymns, the catechism and a book called *The One Mediator* in defence of the Protestant faith. Still in the press were the Psalms, *Pilgrim's Progress* and a Rwanda grammar. One wonders how all this was achieved by a delicate man with a family of six growing children, and no doubt his wife had a great deal to do with it. It was she who drove him and his books and his children over trackless hillsides, and geared the family life to the achievement of his work; all his older children took turns in the holidays in reading aloud the New Testament while he checked his own manuscripts against the English. And then there was his own power of single-minded detachment and his capacity to use every spare moment. A few years later, when they were travelling in Burundi, they came to a broken bridge. He would not have been much use at repairing a bridge; and it struck him that right here was a golden opportunity to translate the Apostle's Creed. "So I hastily unpacked my Rwanda and English prayer books, called the Barundi to me, and it was finished before the bridge was ready to cross." The hymn "There is a happy land", was translated while the car was being filled up with petrol tins in the streets of Gitega.

Even at home the thought of the unfinished tasks never left him and in 1936 he returned alone, a great sacrifice for a man so delicate, so absent-minded, so dependent in practical matters on his wife, so deeply loving and bound to his children. His goal was the whole Bible for Rwanda, but he soon discovered that the people of Burundi needed their own version. However, that belongs to a later chapter.

In collaboration with a team, he started on the Book of Ruth and the Pentateuch with his untiring thoroughness. He spent hours on the anatomical details of the Levitical sacrifices, visiting the hospital and even hurrying out to watch the skinning of a goat, where he finally verified the word for the caul of the liver. He spent further hours poring over books on Rwanda birds, and he had the help of his faithful Samsoni and Monsieur Honoré, and some of the Seventh Day Adventist missionaries. By June 1937 he wrote triumphantly, "The Rwanda Pentateuch is finished and I am back in Burundi. It has been a great joy and privilege to do this work in Rwanda and I have the happiest memories of it. To see stories like the brazen serpent and the story of Balaam take shape in the Rwanda language; to read such a chapter as Numbers 11 to an enthralled audience and see them appreciate to the full the ingratitude of the Israelites, and see them struck with the majesty of God; such things are experiences to remember all one's life, and one can never cease to thank God for being allowed to take part in such a work. But it has been done at a heavy price, for if the time I had spent on the Rwanda Pentateuch had been given to Burundi, the whole New Testament might have been finished before my return home."

It was a year of joy and sorrow. His wife and Lindesay joined him in May, but by August he was on his way home again, torn in half by the needs of his family and the needs of Burundi. "Only eight or nine months more would have meant the completion of the New Testament for Burundi," he wrote, "but we have felt there was nothing else we could do, so here we are on the ship, very sad."

"So teach us to number our days that we may apply our hearts unto wisdom," was his prayer all along. He intended to come back, but he seemed to know that he must number his days and use every hour to the full. "There is only barely time," he wrote, and again, "the time is very short for what needs to be done. Pray that Samsoni and I may keep well; there is no margin of time for illness."

5

Over the Border

Two years had passed since the first team of evangelists had gone over the border into Rwanda to set up their lonely outposts on the British Bufumbira (eastern) strip. But the division of the country proved impossible and in 1924 the territory was handed back to Belgium, leaving the infant Mission once more on foreign territory.

Dr Stanley Smith travelled to Kigali, the capital, to ask the Belgian Resident for permission to remain. Roman Catholic opposition was strong and the whole future of the Mission was at stake. He opened his *Daily Light* and read, "Fear not, little flock, for it is your Father's good pleasure to give you the kingdom," and he went confidently to the interview. The Resident was most friendly and sanctioned the continuation of the work and the establishment of a foreign mission.

The British withdrew. The railway project was abandoned. Thousands of pounds were wasted, but God had used these events to open a door for the Gospel and it has never been shut since.

Geoffrey Holmes was the chosen pioneer who set out on his motor-bike to tour eastern Rwanda. He stayed there for three months visiting the evangelists, whom he found discouraged, homesick, all but overcome but still hanging on. He camped in his little tent and a tremendous mutual attraction sprang up between him and the Tutsi chiefs. "How anyone with a changed heart could help falling in love with the Tutsi is beyond me," he wrote. "A race of gentlemen with beautiful physique, undoubtedly as fine as the world produces, keen on games and sport, but proud, arrogant and cruel; scornful of anything that savors of manual labour, and yet so superstitious and deceivable, in spite of great mental abilities. One longs that they should get a vision of the Crucified."

He soon found a foothold at the Royal Court at Nyanza and became friendly with the King. The British army athlete challenged the famous royal runners and was beaten by only a foot, which simply delighted His Majesty. "I asked him to show me some jumping," wrote Holmes, "but the chap who beat me running, did about six foot, seven inches. I did not compete."

He came back from his tour sure of his calling, and in July 1925, Leonard Sharp and Mr Roome of the British and Foreign Bible Society, went down with him to approve the site he had chosen for his new mission station. Gahini hill was a good choice. It stands on the east end of Lake Muhazi at the junction of roads going north, south, east and west, with the lake itself a fine potential waterway, twenty-five miles long, through the hills westward. By September he had settled. His tent was the first centre of the Mission in Rwanda.

There were endless possibilities for advance and the young man, burning to build and expand and evangelize, must have felt that the sky was the limit; but financially they were in no position to start an advance programme and so in 1926 Dr Stanley Smith went home to confer with the C.M.S. With God-given courtesy and tact on both sides, the Ruanda General and Medical Mission became a separate, independent auxiliary of the C.M.S. The story of its inception is best told in Dr Stanley Smith's own words.

"From the very beginning the Ruanda Mission has been sustained by the gifts and the prayers of a devoted band called 'Friends of Ruanda', but by 1926 certain factors led to the formation of a Home Council, which was to direct the Mission as an auxiliary of the C.M.S. The first factor was the rapid expansion of the work involving commitments which our original band of friends could not be expected to meet and for which the C.M.S. could not accept the responsibility or cost of advance; yet advance was imperative. A further factor was that the evangelical world was being convulsed by controversies over fundamental beliefs, and the Mission had, from its inception, been clear as to its stand on the great foundation truths which were everywhere being assailed. It was felt to be vital for the continuance of the work that safeguards should be given, so that the witness of the Mission might be united and unchanging. The Mission believed that recruits and funds, which might not be attracted to the C.M.S., could be found if it could be given an assured position. The proposal was sympathetically received by the General Secretary of the C.M.S., the Rev W. Wilson Cash, and passed by the Executive Committee.

"A meeting was convened by the Rev W. W. Martin in Emmanuel Vicarage, South Croydon, at which a number of evangelical leaders agreed to form the Home Council of the Mission. The first meeting of the Council was held in Holy Trinity Vicarage, Tunbridge Wells, at the invitation of Canon Stather Hunt.

"Three principles were affirmed in the Constitution of the Ruanda General and Medical Mission.

1. The Ruanda Council and the missionaries of the R.G.M.M. stand for the complete inspiration of the whole Bible as being, and not merely containing, the Word of God.
2. Their determination is to proclaim full and free salvation in simple faith in Christ's atoning death upon the Cross.
3. They are satisfied that they have received from C.M.S. full guarantees to safeguard the future of the R.G.M.M. on Bible, Protestant and Keswick lines.

"The whole future development of the Mission turned, under God's goodness, on the faithful backing and service given by the Council, and especially its permanent staff. The Rev H. Earnshaw-Smith and Mr Reginald Webster shared the secretarial work of the Mission until in 1931, Mr Webster became Organizing Secretary with the office at 4 Aldermanbury Avenue."

But all this is running far ahead of Geoffrey Holmes, living in meagre style in his tent on Gahini hill. He was not, however, alone. He took with him a man prepared by God for the work. Some thirty years earlier, a family fled from the Gahini district in a local riot. They travelled north, settled in Uganda on the plains of Ankole and bought a herd of long-horned cattle. Little Kosiya longed to go to school, but was not allowed to. He had to look after the cows instead, but he was a spirited little boy and, hearing that his father had gone to pay his respects to the Prime Minister of Ankole, he followed him and turned up in the crowd. A seven-year-old boy in such a company was unusual, and the Prime Minister noticed the bright little face and called him out. "Why are you not in school?" he asked playfully, and Kosiya explained that that was just where he longed to be, and orders were given to his embarrassed father to enter him at once for the Mission primary school at Mbarara. He did well, and a few years later he was noticed again, this time by Bishop Willis, who recognized in him unusual qualities of tenacity and leadership. The Bishop paid his fees to Mbarara High School and from there he went to King's College, Budo, and emerged with the best education Uganda could give, and speaking fluent English.

Kosiya could have gone far materially, but in 1924 Dr Stanley Smith visited the college and appealed for volunteers to go as missionaries to Rwanda. To the others it was a call to a wild, strange land, but to young Kosiya Shalita it was a call back to his own country to preach the Gospel in his own mother tongue. He left all and followed, joined Geoffrey Holmes in his tent on the Gahini hillside only twenty-eight miles from his own birthplace, and started a school for boys. "It is wonderful how God chooses people many years before He tells them what He wants them to do," he wrote. "Who knew that I was going to tell my own people about God? God knew, and He took me out of my country for that purpose."

The Rev Herbert S. Jackson, who soon joined them, seems to have been less well prepared, at least on the medical side, for what was in store for him. A soldier in the first World War, the horrors of the trenches appalled him. "This chaos of mud, blood and death, convinced me that the world needed God." So, in 1919, he went to Cambridge and was ordained. During his first curacy at Eastbourne, he heard Dr Stanley Smith's appeal for Rwanda and, in January 1926, he pitched his tent next to Geoffrey Holmes on Gahini hill.

He came into a hive of activity. Geoffrey Holmes was a big man and did everything in a big way. He had a big voice for issuing orders and he had big ideas; he built big houses and loved hunting big game. He had planted a garden half a mile long, and thousands of trees. Everything moved with military precision and extreme efficiency. His boys loved him and never forgot him, and his workmen respected him and feared him. Bert Jackson, however, saw the other side of the picture and was not entirely happy. What did all this activity look like to the local African, watching with fascinated alarm from his kraal and banana patch?

"Some of the men are volunteers sent by local chiefs," he wrote. "They would far rather sit about in their kraals and do nothing. No doubt we appear an awful nuisance, if nothing worse. We come and settle on their land; we make them sell us eggs and milk; we put up buildings and make gardens and roads on what was once their grazing ground; and we make them work. Very good for them, but highly distasteful. Our difficulty is to get them to see that we are really here for their good. Later, when we are not too tied to the work, we shall be able to show loving sympathy to these people. Until then, they may get an impression which it will be hard to break down later. Pray for the needed tact and wisdom."

They made a good team. The one with his drive and the

other with his gentleness; and Kosiya Shalita, acting as go-between and interpreter, often poured oil on the troubled waters of the astonished local population. As well as brick-making, tree felling, building, gardening, learning the lan-gauge, chasing the stray hippo out of the garden, teaching, preaching, preparing baptism candidates and supervising work-men, Bert Jackson found himself in charge of a flourishing primitive dispensary. He became immensely popular and, with six different medicines, some disinfectant, tooth forceps, surgi-cal needles and thread, a very little knowledge and still less language, he was soon seeing about a hundred patients a day. His lack of language often wasted much time. "I remember a man coming in clasping his tummy and groaning with pain," he wrote. "I pressed him here and tapped him there, took pulse and temperature and could find nothing wrong. I was about to give him a dose of salts, and said, 'Open your mouth.' 'Oh, no,' he said, 'it's not *me*; it's my brother over the hill.'"

But he wrestled bravely with jiggers, fevers, ticks, malaria, yaws, leprosy and sores, as well as the care of the churches; and it was a great day when he baptized the first little group. Later, in 1926, his task was lightened by the gift of a motor-boat in which to speed the length and breadth of Lake Muhazi and visit the out stations; also by a visit from Dr Stanley Smith, who brought a team of teachers and skilled workmen from Kabale and was amazed at the progress and development at Gahini and the outlying stations.

"At Gatsibu (one of these 'stations') we found a pastor and his wife doing a medical missionary work for which we could praise God. We found about a hundred sick and crippled at-tending daily for treatment, after which all gathered to hear the word of love preached with a zeal and faithfulness which is bearing eternal fruit. Gahini dispensary is doing a great work under the personal supervision of the Rev H. S. Jackson, and now two trained assistants from Kabale, Erisa and Paulo. Over a hundred sick are seen daily, and there would be many in-patients but for lack of accommodation. You will rejoice to know that the foundations of the new hospital at Gahini are finished."

And away back in England, God had again prepared the doctor who arrived before the new hospital was even roofed. John Church was the son of a Cambridge parson and one of ten children. A keen sportsman and yachtsman, he was converted at a beach service in Whitby while still a student, but it was not until he was threatened with T.B. that he gave his life wholly and unreservedly to God. After a sudden, severe lung haemorrhage, faced with the prospect of early death, he looked up to God and made a vow. "I will surrender every bit of my life and quit absolutely all sin and go as a missionary if You will heal me," and God in His patient mercy accepted the prayer and he was healed.

Joe, as he is always called, kept to his part of the promise with all the strength and enthusiasm of his strong, warm personality. Once, in a book, he had read these words, "If Christianity is anything, it is everything," and they became his working slogan. In 1922 he and some friends formed the Cambridge University Missionary Band in Clarence Foster's rooms, and spared no pains to capture missionaries on furlough. Little did some of those tired individuals realize at what a merciless judgment board they were sitting. To the deeply consecrated, highly inexperienced young men, you either had "it" or you didn't; and how many an earnest, sincere missionary would have been amazed and sorrowful to know that his visit had only one result, to make the members of that little group pray with fierce entreaty, "Lord, never let me become like that. Keep my vision clear and my zeal red-hot. Oh Lord, never, never let me get cold."

Joe Church's call came in 1925 with clear certainty when he heard Dr Stanley Smith speak at one of their famous missionary breakfasts. His text was, "It is not well. This is a day of good tidings and you hold your peace. Go and tell." He heard, that day, of the land of five million inhabitants with no mission hospital and, with characteristic zeal, he made his preparations to go. He took a special course in skin and venereal diseases at Bart's (St Bartholomew's) and studied tropical medicine in Brussels. In 1927 he made a last deputation tour and enlisted five hundred prayer partners. His support was guaranteed by the C.I.C.C.U. (Cambridge Inter-Collegiate Christian Union), who made him their special missionary. He also became engaged to Miss Decima Tracey, a clever young medical student and the tenth child of a Devonshire doctor.

He reached Kampala in 1927 and was instantly conscious of strain and dissension. All the elements that had caused the division between the theologically conservative Bible Churchman's Missionary Society and the C.M.S. were present, and certainly there was reason for concern. He stood by the graves of Mackay and Hannington and other pioneers of the faith and watched crowds flocking up the hill to Namirembe Cathedral, and he knew, because people told him, that many of these baptized, third-generation Christians had gone back into witchcraft and polygamy.

Joe set off on his motor-bike for Kabale thinking long, deep thoughts. It was cheering, after two days, to round a bend on those almost unclimbable Kigezi hills and see his old friend, Len Sharp, standing in the road in a Trinity blazer, surrounded by a crowd of smart little schoolboys. He was introduced to the team, busy, cheerful and welcoming, but under all the bright preparations for Christmas and the kindness showered upon him, he was aware of uneasy questions rising in his own mind.

He attended the early service on Christmas morning and watched the hundreds of people, clad in damp goatskins, stealing in through the blanket of mist, crowding the dank church, rejoicing at the story of the wise men and the shepherds, and going back like happy children into the mists of ignorance and superstition. Was there any real change of heart or life, any real conviction of sin? The numbers were far too great for anyone to make a true assessment. Besides, there were other questions that seemed to loom large. How much of the traditional English Christmas should be introduced to this primitive company of Christians? How far should the full Anglican Liturgy be introduced into this young Church on Kabale hill? Was it right to urge these people to believe in a God, and put their faith in Christ, about whom they knew so little?

"Don't take sides," said somebody to Joe on the first night, and his reply was the result of those uncompromising C.I.C.C.U. years. "There is only one side." "You will understand later," said the missionary and left him, but he did not understand. His exuberant spirits and extreme interest in sport and in his new surroundings hid the turmoil in his heart, and perhaps no one, at first, realized it was there.

"I thought him a very immature young man," said an older missionary. "He always seemed to be chasing butterflies."

He caught his first glimpse of Rwanda on safari with Dr Stanley Smith in April, when they crossed Lake Bunyoni in narrow, dug-out canoes. They followed the elephant tracks through bamboo forests and reached the Kanaba gap and looked out over the breath-taking panorama of the Bufumbira volcanoes. But his actual departure was on 22nd June 1928 when he left Kabale on a motor-bike in company with a pet monkey and an Airedale puppy called Cuss. It was the end of the rainy season and all the world was green and gold, with fields of sunflowers and cassia trees in full bloom. He was happy, going to start his own hospital at last with a fine team from Kabale, including Yosiya Kinuka, coming down shortly to join him. The prospects were bright.

It was a great surprise as he neared Gahini almost to collide with Geoffrey Holmes, who was travelling in the opposite direction—somewhat painfully because of the enormous ulcer on his leg. Holmes had decided to leave Gahini to the younger man, and also to give Joe the benefit of his own house to live in. He was off again, sick and alone, to pitch his tent on new territory, and Joe must have felt strangely bereft as that soldierly figure, the very embodiment of strength and purpose, rattled off along the track and disappeared. Besides, he was appalled by the filth and misery and obvious hunger of the people he had passed on the journey. Steep and bare rose Gahini hill and the thought crossed his mind, "Why have I come to this desert spot?" Then he saw Kosiya Shalita running down the hill to meet him, and he was comforted.

His first few hours at Gahini confirmed his worst fears. The rains had failed in Rwanda. The dry season was beginning and famine was certain. Stores were running out and Bert Jackson, haggard and weary, was bringing in loads of beans in the motor-boat from across the lake. Refugees camped all round the Mission in grass shelters and as he bumped up the hill, covered with dirt from his hundred-mile drive, the sick were waiting for him huddled under the walls of his unfinished hospital. In his own bedroom, shortly after his arrival, he operated on an old chief with multiple abcesses.

Those first months were a sort of nightmare, when Joe Church and Bert Jackson and their devoted African helpers kept going simply because it was quite impossible ever to stop. The famine threatened to wipe out the eastern Rwanda population and hundreds and hundreds dragged their way to the Uganda border, or died on the way. Within a fortnight of arrival Joe had admitted fifteen patients into the unroofed hospital, and was preaching to them by interpretation, but he felt almost desperate. The buildings were falling down; his foot and knee were severely infected; no letter had reached him from Decie for two months; and above all, the famine grew worse every day.

In November Dr Stanley Smith came down with his wife and family to live for a time in the famine-stricken area. What his presence meant to the two exhausted, bewildered young pioneers can only be guessed, the more that both had been recently mauled by leopards and Joe's life had only been saved by the courage of Kosiya Shalita. All the team concentrated together on the medical refugee work. The unfinished hospital buildings were crammed to capacity. The Government responded to their appeal for supplies, and they quickly became a distribution centre.

"It is impossible for me to describe the terrible spectacle presented by starving patients who flock to the hospital," wrote Joe. "They crawl to us from miles round, and by the time they arrive, have scarcely sufficient strength in their shrunken, shrivelled bodies to hold out their hands and say, 'The famine kills me, food, food.' Many are covered with ulcers, filthily dirty, their toes and fingers rotting with jiggers. As they lie on the ground with the flies crawling over them, one's heart is almost broken when one thinks that for these almost inhuman beings, Christ died. Yesterday I came upon a woman huddled up amongst bricks and rubbish, almost dead. One cannot go far in any direction without seeing corpses by the roadside; and conditions at the hospital are ghastly and very difficult to deal with. We have had to open our doors to a flood of starving, diseased people. The offices are food stores and the wards and verandahs are full of desperate people, who must stay with us or go away to steal or die. It is impossible to keep the place clean. Dysentery has broken out, and people are actually dying from jiggers. They burrow into the fingers, toes, elbows, knees and buttocks, until the children are absolutely helpless, unable to feed themselves properly. We need hundreds of safety-pins to give these wretched people, with which to extract the jiggers. Please send some."

They were months of indelible horror as the desperate, stealing, starving hordes, stumbling on towards the Uganda border, made Gahini hill their wayside inn, to rest or to die. The ground was too hard and parched to bury their dead and there was the putrid, haunting smell of death in the very winds that blew. Jackals howled in the garden at night and the team woke in the morning dreading what they might find: a naked corpse half devoured and a tiny starving child clinging to its mother's lifeless body.

Joe was numbed, exhausted, horrified. The Stanley Smiths had to leave before Christmas and the famine was still at its height. He had leaned heavily on Algie's optimistic faith and experience, and as well as sharing the burden of the medical work with him, his friendship had meant, and was always to mean, a great deal to him. With a heart like lead, Joe watched the car drive off down the hill and disappear into the folded hills around Lake Muhazi. He was broken down by ill health and poor nutrition and by the terrible responsibility of the whole situation; haunted by fears of the future, deeply troubled by wrong relationships in the church and a sense of failure. "Surely", he wrote, "there must be a deeper place of rest in Jesus; a deeper place of understanding of the victorious life."

It was the darkest hour before the dawn.

6

Breath of Life

In spite of the departure of the Stanley Smiths, Joe was not left uncared for. A few weeks previously Mrs Wilkinson, mother of the Rev L. F. E. Wilkinson, later Chairman of the Ruanda Council, arrived at Gahini. Universally known as Mrs Winnie, she settled in at once, quite undeterred by the famine, collapsing buildings, jiggers and complete lack of language, and proceeded to do what she could with kindly common sense and practical efficiency.

She mothered the two harassed young bachelors, distributed tons of food, coped with the cows, obtained milk for starving babies and took a number of little dying orphan children into her home and cared for them as her own. Her own health broke down after a time, and she had to go home in 1931, but Mrs Winnie, with her loving Christian spirit and imperturbable temperament, was God's gift to Gahini just then.

The terrible parched months dragged on and death lurked at their doors day and night. In March, Joe became desperate and travelled to Kampala resolved to make the world acquainted with Rwanda's anguish. Backed by Bishop Willis and Dr Albert Cook, he wrote an article for the Uganda press, describing the horrors of the famine and appealing for help.

It was as though he had dropped a spark on to dry timber. Unable to stand the conflagration caused by his action, he hurried back to Rwanda to face the first results, a very angry Belgian Resident whose leave had been cancelled by head-quarters at Brussels with orders to look into the scandal and

E
65

send immediate reports. In fact, the whole Belgian population was outraged by the implied criticism of their local government; and added to the nightmare of the famine, the fear of being expelled from the country hung over Joe like a black cloud. Reports that *The Times* in London was publishing a famine appeal and that the Rwanda situation was now world news, did little to cheer him. He was at the end of his tether. The rains had come, but as yet there was no harvest and on some days as many as twenty emaciated refugees died of hunger and exposure on the premises. He wrote to Decie:

"I'm searching my life day by day to conquer all sins that may be stopping communication with the Lord. Out here, the Devil is twice as strong and subtle as he is at home."

He longed for Algie's cheerful courage and sanity, and sending a message ahead to summon him, he set out to meet him. Algie came at once and they camped that night in a windy hut by the roadside a hundred miles north of Gahini and, like Jonathan and David, Algie "strengthened his hands in God". Algie radiated comfort and good news. Money for the relief of Rwanda was pouring in from all over the world and materially the outlook was bright. The tremendous spiritual battle seemed less overwhelming as they prayed about it together and Joe returned to Gahini strengthened and cheered. Two hundred and fifty thousand pounds was donated by the Minister of Colonies; a stream of gifts came in as a result of the appeal in *The Times* and within a month or so the country was transformed. Engineers from Switzerland and Italy were forging ahead building roads for the transport of relief supplies throughout the length and breadth of Rwanda and Burundi, and the feet of God's messengers soon followed them—God's hour for advance was about to arrive and there in the desert were the highways, prepared.

But Joe did not realize the full import of all this just then. He was too taken up with his own immediate problems and conflicts. "Just for the moment," wrote Bert Jackson, "all our wonderful plans for the Church and the water supply are held up as we can think of nothing but food. Every ounce of strength is being put into cultivation. The getting of food is the be-all and end-all of the people's existence. Even those to whom we have given a daily ration of food, are sometimes caught digging up our poor little crops of sweet potatoes before they are ripe."

By June the country was green again. The famine was virtually over and men began to lift up their heads, but the Gahini staff who had worked so heroically and selflessly through the months of crisis were at their lowest ebb. They were flagging physically and spiritually. They needed to relax, but Joe would allow no relaxation. Though no linguist himself, the preaching had to go on. He was as relentless with them as he was with himself, expecting them to set standards and ideals for which they were not spiritually ready. His rosy vision of "every man an evangelist" and the church and hospital working hand in hand as a happy team was an excellent one, but the members of the team were hungry, discontented and exhausted. Things came to a head one day when a group of African workers suddenly appeared before him with their uniforms folded, and their belongings in tidy bundles on their heads. "We are going," they announced.

It was probably a threat, a gesture, an attempt to parley, but their leader was as strained and exhausted and spiritually drained as they were. "All right, good-bye," he replied bitterly, and they went as silently as they had come. It was a defeat of the first order.

But there were encouragements. One day, when the sense of failure and defeat became almost too heavy to bear, Joe walked twenty miles along the edge of Lake Muhazi. He spent the night with a friend and climbed the hill at daybreak, sitting for a long time in the shade of an umbrella acacia tree watching the morning mists breaking over the lake. One by one veiled objects became visible and stood out distinctly and individu-

67

ally: the crimson of the erythrina tree; a lithe black figure rhythmically plying his hoe; a dug-out canoe skimming across the smooth, shining water; fold upon fold of shimmering mountain. And then the mists were scattered altogether and the whole land lay bathed in sunshine. He prayed passionately for the scattering of the mists of superstition and sin and the shining forth of the light of the Gospel, and the site of the beautiful spreading acacia tree seemed like holy ground to be claimed for God. He lost no time in cycling the ten miles to Kigali, the capital, signing the necessary documents and buying the patch of land. The Christians built a church around the central tree trunk, the huge branches shading the thatched roof, and Ndera hill was the first Gospel foothold near the capital.

Something had happened to him under that old acacia tree. He went back with a deeper desire to know God better, a passionate longing that others also should come to know Him, and a determination to explore yet further into the spiritual realm. "One can specialize in medical research, surgery or translation," he wrote, "but what is the priority in it all? What is the Kingdom of God that we have to seek first in order that all these things may be added to us? Let us think of the thing that we really love most and then ask God to excel it with His love."

There were signs of new life round them everywhere. The land was green again and the harvests were sprouting. Mrs. Winnie's little famine orphans were beginning to look like healthy children and the boys' and girls' schools were filling up again. As though drawn by some new spirit, Christians were meeting together at dawn to pray, crouching on Joe's verandah while the sky was still starry, and there was a strange new hunger for the Word of life, too. Work stopped every afternoon and a crowd of about a hundred and fifty to two hundred, carpenters, masons, nurses, patients and relatives, all assembled quietly for Bible study. The talks given at that time were later

published in a book, *Every Man a Bible Student*, a publication
that ran into seventy thousand copies.

But the Devil was contending every step and Joe, striving
desperately to keep up with these new claims, was beset by
self-hatred, despair and anxiety. He had failed his language
exam and Decie was unwell. Could he ever ask her to come
and share conditions such as he had been through? And, in
any case, would the Medical Board ever pass her? In September
he wrote to her, "I think in many ways this is one of the
heaviest, blackest moments of my life. The Lord is as real as
ever, but I cannot see an inch ahead. I often feel my witness
for Christ must be almost nil. I am just trying all the more to
give the Lord absolutely everything, and then to wait for His
guiding hand. I can offer you nothing but my love, my protection and the work, and to share with me my ambitions for the
Master."

Mercifully, it was time for his holiday, worn out as he was,
and he came to Kampala with only one resolve—to find the
real secret of victory over sin. It was here that God took
charge. He was climbing Namirembe hill on his way to the
great cathedral, when a young African named Simeoni
Nsibambi stopped him. "I heard you speak at a Bible class here,
in March, about surrendering all to Jesus," he said. "I have
done so and have found great joy in the Lord, but I have
wanted to see you ever since. There is still something missing
in me and in the Uganda Church. Can you tell what it is?"
Simeoni was known to Joe because his young brother, Blasio,
was their schoolmaster at Gahini, and Simeoni, a rich man in
government service, had been the means of the boy's conversion. Now the two men went home together and pored over
their Bibles for hours on end. With the aid of Schofield's notes,
they traced the teaching on the Holy Spirit and the victorious
life right through the Bible, and suddenly all the answers he
had known for so long in theory blazed into reality for Joe. He
wrote of his experience to the C.I.C.C.U. "I have been feeling

lately there can be nothing to stop a real outpouring of the Holy Spirit in Rwanda now except our own lack of sanctification as members of the Mission. There could be a revival of the Uganda Church if there was someone who could come, Spirit filled, and point these thousands of nominal Christians to the victorious life. Pray for a real conviction of sin and then the outpouring of the Spirit Himself will follow. God met with me. He gave me no special gift. The only special gift is the experience of the transforming vision of the Risen Jesus, Himself."

Both men were transformed. Nsibambi could not contain the joy of his new discovery and Joe was criticized and reprimanded. "What have you done to Nsibambi?" inquired one indignantly. "Rushing round and asking everyone if they are saved! He's just left my gardener!" Others admitted a work of the Holy Spirit, but it was not generally considered suitable for Uganda. It would be far too upsetting and revolutionary. "Go back to Rwanda," some advised Joe. "The Africans are not ready for this sort of thing yet." Perplexed and chilled, he sought out Algie and once again the older man's simple, sanctified common sense steadied him. "If this happens when you ask God for a new filling of the Holy Spirit," said Algie, "then you must trust that what follows is His will."

Joe went back to Gahini a new man, sure that God was going to work on their behalf, and he was not disappointed. Almost immediately there were three notable conversions in the hospital. One was a chief, who having yielded his life to Christ, asked at once, "How long before I can be baptized?" "You can be baptized now," was the answer; and kneeling on the grass the once proud chief prayed, "Lord, I have heard Thy words and I have believed. I am like a blind man. Open my eyes that I may see." Out at a branch dispensary there was another conversion in answer to many prayers, when old Karakezi, a high-class Tutsi whose son had died a believer in hospital, came out of heathendom and accepted Christ.

70

Something had happened. Gone was the old complacency and that pleasant, outward conformity to the white man's standard, while one quietly lived one's own life behind the scenes. Truth had suddenly become important. Men lay awake at night grieving over their sins and hypocrisies, and stolen goods began to be returned; small sums of money, a hoe, a razor blade. Few remained indifferent and those who dared not face the light of the Spirit of God were utterly wretched and wanted to run away from it; and none more so than Yosiya Kinuka, Joe's trusted hospital dresser.

As already mentioned, Yosiya had first heard the Gospel as a boy of fourteen when, covered with sores and ulcers, he had been treated in Kabale hospital. Christianity had brought him compassion, health, friendship, and later, education and a good job with Joe, a man he loved and respected. Christianity was obviously an excellent thing and he went over to it with all his heart and was baptized and confirmed. Adopting its principles and practices, he had worked valiantly and efficiently throughout the famine. But now, he was beginning to realize that there was another side to Christianity, a disturbing, costly side that asked more of him than he was prepared to give and yet gave him no rest if he refused.

His misery was poisoning him and he was beginning to hate his master. Why should he be forced into this everlasting preaching when he had nothing to say and his whole experience belied all that he taught? He bullied his wife and quarrelled with his fellow workers and subordinates. There was Paulo, for instance. They hated each other and their hatred affected the atmosphere of the whole hospital. Joe, Blasio and Kosiya Shalita prayed for him day after day, but there was no immediate break. His holiday was due and he decided to go and never return.

Although Joe paid his fare to Uganda on condition that he went to see Nsibambi, Yosiya did not tell him his true intentions. After all, they had built up the hospital and had been through the famine together. Their ties were strong. But he thought that he was turning his back on Gahini for ever when he set off over the mountains to Uganda.

"But whither shall I flee from Thy Spirit?" He had escaped Joe, but he could not escape the restlessness. "All things betray him who betrayest Me," and Yosiya found no satisfaction anywhere. At last, in despair, he travelled up to Kampala and called on Nsibambi and poured out his woes—that he had been ill-treated, underpaid, the hospital was rotten, the doctor impossible. But he received no sympathy. Nsibambi was inexorable. "The hospital is rotten because you are rotten," he stated simply. "You need to open your heart to Jesus."

Angry and disappointed, Yosiya left him and got a lift in a night lorry. All through the dark hours he sat, huddled and wakeful, and the wheels turning on the red earth tracks seemed to grind out the refrain hundreds of times over, "The hospital is rotten because you are rotten. You must open your heart to Jesus."

So that was the secret. Not the acceptance of the white man's religion and corresponding change of behaviour, but a heart wide open to God, transformed by the light and love and sweetness of the character of Jesus. All these weary years and he had never known it, but he experienced it then. "The Lord has forgiven me," he announced to his wife. "Can you forgive me?"

He came back to Gahini alight with the joy of forgiveness. There was still much to be forgiven and put right, but Joe and Blasio and Kosiya received him as a brother. These Africans were no longer servants whose job it was to please the white man, but a team of brethren together, all serving one Master, Christ; set free from their old servility and hypocrisy to be their real selves. It was a new, untried relationship and it evoked some criticism, but the team knew that the bonds had been forged by Christ and they rejoiced.

It was like a tender, spiritual springtime. Yosiya went

straight to Paulo, his old enemy, and Paulo broke down completely, overcome by such loving humility. "Beat me a hundred strokes with a hippo hide for all my sins and hatred," he cried, weeping bitterly and he, too, opened his heart to Jesus.

Joy was so great that it could not be confined. They must tell it abroad and, one by one, they went out like God's troubadours, singing aloud of forgiveness and love. Paulo left his wife in the girls' school and asked leave to go and preach Christ near his old home in the market of Kigali. Erifazi went east to the dreaded, mosquito-ridden border of Tanganyika (as it was then) and God's blessing went with them, and wherever they came men were smitten with a divine discontent. Under the dead leaves of hypocrisy, respectability and formality, the living shoots of sincerity, reality and truth were starting to spring up. The outwardly successful decade of nominal Christianity was over and everywhere men were beginning to hunger and thirst for the living God.

7

Leprosy

By 1930 a number of new missionaries had joined the Ruanda Mission. Miss Forbes, Miss King and the Rev E. Lawrence Barham were settled at Kigezi. Mr Cecil Verity and Miss Dora Skipper had joined the staff at Gahini. Financially, God had blessed them and in 1929 the Ruanda Mission had become completely self-supporting. The spirit of new zeal and joy that had quickened Gahini was beginning to spring up in other churches, too. The time for advance was ripe.

In the hospital at Kabale, the ward for leprosy patients was overflowing and many had to be turned away, and it was their plight that perhaps most saddened the Sharps on their safaris through the villages. "The majority are poor, filthy and helpless, and some young children are alive with vermin and jiggers. Two were covered in ulcers from head to foot, their poor little legs doubled under them so they will never be able to walk. They were afraid of their own people, so you can imagine their terror at the sight of a white person. Another was smothered from head to foot with large patches of leprosy; another had her poor old face eaten away."

Two years before, Dr Sharp had stood on the top of a ridge a thousand feet high a few miles from Kabale, and looked far below him at Lake Bunyoni, its blue inlets winding in and out of the folded hills. Not far from the mainland lay a deserted island, the island of his dreams, but being Dr Sharp he was not content to dream. He drew up a practical plan, roughly as follows:

1. We will buy the island of Bwama lying off the shore of Lake Bunyoni. It is only six miles from Kabale and there is a good motor road connecting us with the Lake.

2. On this island we will build a leprosy hospital, with accommodation for fifty in-patients and equipped for treating a large number of out-patients.

3. Attached to the hospital there will be a model village or colony where most patients would live and attend as out-patients.

4. A missionaries' house would be required for two resident ladies one, at least, of whom must be a trained nurse. These, with African Christian staff, would care for the sick and find a unique opportunity for Christian work in the villages.

5. Leprosy patients would be selected after a full census of all such families at Kigezi. All patients wishing to come would be allowed to do so, with their families, and other cases who could be cured or who are a danger to others, would be persuaded to do so.

How was it that such a beautiful island should be overgrown, deserted and uncultivated? Its history was sinister and violent and most people feared the place. It had been connected for years with the heathen cult of a female spirit called Nyabingi and a powerful witch-doctor had lived on the island, who claimed to control rain, fire, disease and death. When he beat his drum, his adherents would collect from the surrounding hills and row across with gifts to appease the evil spirit; sheep, goats, pots of beer, terrified girls. Far into the night one could hear the beating of drums and stamping of feet as the drunken orgy reached frenzy pitch, and so much misery and fear was engendered by this witch-doctor that in 1929 the Government intervened and arrested him and forbade his followers to return to the island. So it became a deserted spot, haunted by fear and memories of evil, shunned by all men.

But our God delights to raise up ruined foundations and

plant gardens in the wilderness and "make the valley of Achor a door of hope", and this was the island that the Government leased to Dr Sharp. In 1930 building started and the Lake Bunyoni Leprosy Settlement began to take shape. The Government of Uganda gave substantial grants. Scrub and jungle were cleared, paths were made, and a number of huts were built for the first patients while building started on the hospital. A bungalow was erected for the English nursing sisters, Miss Langley and Miss Horton. Quite quickly the twenty-five patients from the hospital at Kabale were cajoled, somewhat unwillingly, into their new premises and Dr Sharp's dream had become a reality.

Bwama! In spite of the dread disease it harboured, it was on the whole a place of beauty and hope. It was never an institution in the ordinary sense of the word for, apart from the permanent hospital inmates, the patients lived in their own huts, bore their children and cultivated their own plots of land on the slopes of the island where the soil was wonderfully rich after having lain fallow for so many years. The peace of the hills enfolded the island. The bays and inlets were strewn with mauve and pink water-lilies, and the soft colours of the reflections were beautiful beyond description. Nobody was obliged to stay. They came because they wanted to get well; and although each year death took its toll, about thirty were discharged as "arrested" cases. But many were loth to go, for they had found a love and care and sympathy on the island which they would never find back in the world.

Miss Langley and Miss Horton were the first of a succession of heroic lady missionaries who gave years of their lives to the service of those suffering from that much feared disease. In these days when many missionaries return home with nervous breakdown due to cultural shock, absence of social life, loneliness and overwork, it is good to remember Evelyn Longley, Grace Mash, Janet Metcalf and Marguerite Barley. They remained for years in that isolated place and, apart from the

Sharps, who came to live on the next island, the ladies had no European companionship beyond each other. They carried enormous medical, spiritual and administrative responsibilities, they dealt with the stench and horror of leprosy and bore the burden of the constant sorrow of hopeless, incurable pain and approaching death. Yet all made their home on the island and retained over the years good physical health, soundness of mind, a gay sense of humour and a holy life of fellowship with God. Perhaps, in dedicating one's life to the sick, one counts the cost more thoroughly beforehand and goes forth without any reserves or backward looks, and then there is no disappointment.

Under Dr Sharp's untiring guidance, they divided the island into villages. Bethany and Samaria were for the untainted and the arrested cases, who for some reason or other could not go home. Around the Bethany school, terraced slopes were cultivated where the children learnt the best methods of agriculture. In Bethlehem they built a home for the healthy babies of patients, where their parents could visit them. In Jericho or Nazareth the contagious patients were housed, with their own school for infected children. Everyone who was at all able to be so, was self-supporting and those who could not cultivate learnt a trade: basket and mat making, pottery, netting, sewing, knitting, carving. All except the very ill cooked their own food.

Two buildings finally dominated the island. The beautifully designed brick hospital, soon to be approached through smooth lawns and trees, and that triumph of architecture on the highest point of the island—the church, cruciform in shape with its seventy-foot tower and spire, and built from bricks made on the island. The windows and doors are arched, and instead of an eastern window there is a beautiful recessed arch behind the communion table. In silver letters on wood the text above the arch reads in the Rukiga language, "Believe on the Lord Jesus Christ and thou shalt be saved," and that on the arch itself, "Emmanuel, God with us." Those present will never forget the great day when the church spire was hoisted, with its cross welded into the metal ball formed by two enamel bowls! The steeple was built inside the tower and eight pieces of scaffolding were built around it to steady it as it went up. The moment for hoisting it came. Dr Sharp gave orders that no one was to speak except himself, and the team of men worked in silence. It was a tense few moments, but all went well. The audience watched and prayed and the steeple rose quietly into its place, pointing upward to God, a landmark for the whole lake.

But we are running ahead. When May Langley and the Sharps started admitting the patients, there were just a two-roomed hospital, a nurses' bungalow and a few huts, and May Langley remembers the first operations performed under a tree. "I wish it were in my power to describe the picture as badly maimed men came up to have pieces of dead bone removed from their diseased feet. There are those who think it is nicer to treat acute sufferers who quickly respond to treatment," she wrote, early on in her career. "But I am so glad that these poor creatures appealed to Christ as they did, because He has set us an example and I am sure that all those who are labouring on their behalf are doing it for Him and He will reward them. We often do more good by our sympathy than by our labours, for is not sympathy love added to experience? I have read in your letters the self-sacrifice that some of you have exercised in working for us as you have done, but remember He sees and knows, and that our Saviour took the long, long road which is the road to Heaven, the road that was wet with tears, difficulties and sorrows, the road that led through loving, human service to the crown of thorns and to the pierced hands; but afterwards there is the reward, His 'Well done, good and faithful servant.'"

They were blessed in their early African colleagues. Some enthusiastic, healthy Christians volunteered to come over from the mainland to help in the schools and hospitals, an act of very deep devotion in those days when the disease was dreaded much more than it is now. Amongst these was Ernesti, who left his home and relatives and came to be head hospital dresser even though he and his wife were terrified of contracting the disease. He won the confidence of all the patients and became a clever bacteriologist. Then there was Nekimiya, a gentle Christ-like boy. His hut was always full of sick people— other than leprosy sufferers—for whom there was no accommodation in hospital. Sooner than send them away, he opened his own home to them and his wife fed them, sometimes as many as six at a time, while they received out-patient treatment. Once, when asked why he did it, he replied, "Is not this the teaching of Jesus?"

Then there was Mary from the northern province of Toro, who came as a teacher straight from school. When her headmistress had mentioned the possibility of catching leprosy, she had replied, "I have thought of it and counted the cost, and I am willing to go for Jesus' sake, and I do not mind, for I believe in the coming of Jesus very soon and then all men will have good bodies." But the majority of their staff were drawn from the sufferer's own ranks, some cured or with their disease arrested, some struggling on until the advanced stages of the illness overcame them. Samwiri, the teacher in the Jericho school, was one of the wrecks of this terrible disease. His eyes were constantly watering and the nerves of his face twitched. He had lost his fingers, but with the stumps of his hands he managed to write neatly on the blackboard, and if anyone could instil knowledge into a child whose mind had been dulled by disease, hunger, and the horror that comes from being an outcast, shunned by all, it was Samwiri. He was a born teacher.

It may seem psychologically unsound for children to be taught by a man so crippled and deformed, but here it was a case of necessity. There were few on the island who had much aptitude for teaching and very few would volunteer from outside, but perhaps Samwiri had a place in the training of these

Leprosy

children that could not have been taken by a fit man. There were many in those classes whose hands and feet were beginning to become deformed and when those children began to think, "How shall I hold a pencil when my fingers are all bent up?" there was Samwiri before them, a living example of one who was overcoming his handicap. As one of the Christian patients once said, "In time of trouble a leprosy patient can best be helped by a fellow sufferer who, in Jesus Christ, is living a truly victorious life. He knows by experience all the pain there is to be suffered, how slow the progress, how despised he will be by others because of this disease that is marked by patches. Only animals have patches, but he also knows that with Jesus to help him, 'all things are possible to him that believeth'."

There are others who accept the scourge with praise, and both hands outstretched as the call of God to service. Dr Adeney tells how, in later years, he was seeing out-patients, "when one of our very best schoolmasters came in to see me. He is a very efficient worker, a most attractive personality and a real man of God. 'What is the matter?' I asked him. 'I'm afraid I have leprosy,' was his reply. On examination, his fears were justified, and I told him so.

"He replied, 'When I was a boy at school, the Lord saved me. I was trained as a schoolmaster and He gave me success in my exams, and two months ago He gave me a Christian wife. Now, He has allowed me to have this disease because He wants me to serve Him among the children who are ill with leprosy.'"

He went off, rejoicing, and later his wife joined him. She found him just the same, surrounded by many patients in the advanced stage of the disease. God had given him joy, strength and victory.

There were difficulties, heartaches, and disappointments, but perhaps in no department of the Ruanda Mission have there been greater triumphs over pain, despair and death than at Bwama. The hospital, for all the heartbreaking sights and

80

Early Travel. Dr A. C. (Algie) Stanley Smith, his wife and family

Looking Back. Dr L. E. S. (Len) Sharp, now retired, reading the C.M.S. magazine which announced the start of the Mission

Getting Alongside. Mrs H. E. Guillebaud with blind Monica and her family

Brothers in Christ. Andrew, a schoolmaster; the Rev Fred Barff, Deputation Secretary 1955–1968; the Rev Yona Kanamuzeyi, martyred 1964

sickening smells, was a happy place. At first the treatment consisted of injections of hydnocarpus oil and local dressings of sores and ulcers, but later the sulphone drugs were used with most encouraging results. Even so, there were many for whom nothing could be done physically.

But so many of them found peace and courage and rest in Jesus. There was a church teacher, dying of lepra fever, every part of his body swollen, unable to move without acute pain, but his face was radiant as he told that those who are well cannot comprehend the peace that Jesus gives to those who suffer. "My body is full of pain," he said, "but my heart is full of peace."

"I see a wrinkled old man," writes Miss Mash, describing the wards, "always praising, though minus hands and feet, shuffling across the ward to speak to a fellow-patient about his Saviour. I see a blind, disfigured woman, bravely testifying to peace of heart which she reveals constantly in love and kindness; and yet another, raising fingerless hands above her head in song, or in a vigorous Gospel message. Again I see a fine church teacher, with a radiant face but a husky voice and twisted fingers that hardly look capable of holding the Bible he loves to expound. Most of these cases are incurable and progressive, but even that is not a cause for great sorrow. 'Even if I do not get better,' said one, 'I am a Christian and in the end I shall go to be with the Lord Jesus and I shall have a new body!' And when a Christian patient does die, the burial of the old diseased body becomes a time of great rejoicing as his friends talk together of his new body. 'It does not yet appear what we we shall be, but we shall be like Him.' 'We shall be changed.' Can there be any more joyful prospect? And the scarred, ravaged faces shine with joy as they gather around an open grave on the quiet shores of the lake and sing their favourite hymns, 'In the sweet bye and bye, we shall meet on that beautiful shore,' and 'There is a happy land'."

But many recover and live to serve God. Yona, the teacher,

lived in Burundi and those who said good-bye to him remember his bright face as he turned to leave for Bwama, facing isolation as a leprosy sufferer, setting out for a four-hundred-mile walk into an unknown country. "Don't pity me," he said, "I am rich. Jesus is with me." And then he added, holding up his Testament, "These are my riches." Fifteen months later, he was back, radiant as ever, praising God for healing.

Great joys and great heartbreaks! The grace and victory of God against the suffering, fear, homesickness and separation that the disease involves. One of the hardest aspects was the segregation of the untainted babies to the crèche where their mothers could see them grow up into healthy, beautiful children, but never again look after them or hold them in their arms. The opposition to this practice was almost insuperable at first, and one sister was horrified when four mothers who, at the weekly inspection were told that their babies had contracted leprosy, clapped their hands with glee. It was wonderful news to them as no one would take their babies away from them now. Gradually, however, as more and more little children with the disease were admitted from the mainland, they began to realize the value of the crèche and to hand over their babies, willingly, albeit with tears.

Then there is the horror of ostracism, of becoming the untouchable, the outcast who, even if announced symptom free, will always be shunned and suspected. This cut deeply into their minds and mentalities, and only the consistent, patient love and companionship of fellow Christians, who desired to live alongside them and called them brothers and sisters in Christ, could eradicate these scars. Sometimes this work was helped immeasurably by some passing touch of understanding, as when the Archbishop of Sydney, Dr Howard Mowll, came to dedicate the new hospital. Miss Metcalf wrote, "It was a pouring wet day and everything had to be two hours late, but it was a never-to-be-forgotten day in the history of the island. The Archbishop shook hands with every single patient; those without fingers, those with bandaged hands, even the badly infectious ones. They were very quiet as each, in absolute astonishment, waited for his or her turn. They still talk about it. 'Think, because of the love of Jesus in his heart, he touched us all. One of our tribe would not have touched us, the despised people, but he, the big man in the Church, did it; not because of himself, but because of the Lord Jesus in his heart.' Afterwards, there was a wonderful service and powerful preaching, but it is that touch which lives on in the hearts of men. 'And Jesus put forth His hand and touched him and said, I will, be thou clean.' "

Bwama Island is no longer a receiving centre for those suffering from leprosy which is not now considered such an infectious disease as before. The recent trend is to treat patients periodically in clinics and visit them in their homes. Pat Gilmer, a nurse from the Middlesex Hospital, goes round in her well-equipped van and searches them out, giving them regular treatment. But Bwama still functions as an eventide home where elderly patients too maimed or too old to start life afresh are visited by Pat and lovingly cared for by African Christians. In 1968 the Island took on a new lease of life as a centre for disabled people to learn trades to enable them to be self-supporting.

8

Northward and Southward

But while Dr Sharp dreamed of his leprosy settlement, and personally supervised the building of it, he had not forgotten Rwanda and his eager, statesmanlike mind was already planning ahead, pushing forward. In the spring of 1929, while home on furlough, he wrote, "After much thought, we all feel that two new mission stations will be required for evangelizing Rwanda, one in the north and one in the southwest. Then with three in Burundi, we ought to aim at five more mission stations. Let us determine, God willing, to open a new station early in 1930."

They had made a careful geographical survey and noted that there were three mission centres (or "stations" as they were called then) run by Belgian Protestants, and two by Seventh Day Adventists, across the centre of Rwanda, but the north and the south were, as yet, completely unevangelized. Monsieur Mazoratti, the Governor, had given them permission to advance, but a new Governor had succeeded him and the consent needed to be ratified. There was very little time between Dr Sharp's return from England and Dr Stanley Smith's departure. Together, the two planned the journey of exploration for the eighth of July, but no reply to their letter to the Governor had arrived. As on other occasions, they set out in faith.

They stayed two nights at Gahini to discuss the building of the new girls' school and, while there, the manager of a firm in Kampala paid them a visit. He mentioned that the new Governor was touring the territory and passing quite close to

Gahini on the way back to the capital that very day. By dint of setting out immediately, the travellers were able to waylay the Governor on the road and he proved most friendly and encouraged them to go ahead. "Who was it", wrote Dr Stanley Smith, "who planned that the Governor from three hundred miles south, the Kampala businessman from three hundred miles north and ourselves from a hundred miles west, should meet at that spot on that one day and so pave the way for our journey of discovery under full official sanction?"

They followed the track of a new motor road leading up into North-west Rwanda, but it was tough going, traversing the highest ridges of the Rwanda plateau. On either side of them rose the northern mountains, interspersed with valleys and hills, thickly populated. They slept in primitive rest camps among the high hills and one single, empty hill-top seemed suitable.

They turned south along the red dirt-tracks through the mountains until it was impossible to take the car any further. At some point between Butare and Nyanza, they struck off up the slopes on foot. When swift tropical darkness fell, they asked for shelter at a chief's hut and prayed that he might not prove hostile. Very quickly they discovered that he was the brother of a much-loved patient and friend, who had become a Christian at Gatsibu and had subsequently died of T.B. For the sake of his brother, the chief was willing to grant them anything they wanted. Together, by the dim glow of a lantern, they read *Daily Light* before lying down to sleep, and God's promise shone out as brightly as the stars above them. "I go to prepare a place for you." Next day they found another empty hill-top and went home, confident and rejoicing, to make applications to the Government.

Permission for both sites was refused, although no particular reason was given. Now, we can look back and realize that God had provided some better thing, but it was puzzling at the time. However, the official sanction still held, and Dr Sharp had heard God's call to advance. So, in November the Sharps and the Guillebauds set out on their second expedition. They soon separated in order to explore further, and the Guillebauds turned north, while the Sharps went on westward.

Those early pioneer wives were very tough. They covered over a thousand miles on that second journey of two-and-a-half weeks and the road surface was as slippery as glass in the mud and rain and the sides precipitous. Decie Church was about six months pregnant, but along with the others she walked the rough thirteen miles to the camp where they slept. The ladies also had the energy to visit the chief's wives that evening and provided great entertainment by letting down their long, abundant hair.

The night was spent at the bottom of Shyira hill and in the morning they climbed the thousand feet to the summit. They stood looking up at the other hills that seemed to make a green wall about them and knew that this was it, the "better thing" that God had provided. Further south the leading of God seemed equally clear. A small remnant of primeval forest, seven thousand feet in altitude, had just been reached by the new road which was being built to the Congo border, twenty-five miles from Butare. On a bare ridge just off the road, overlooking a vast valley, stood a clump of trees. And once again they knew that Kigeme hill was to be claimed for God.

But once again permission for both sites was refused.

Why? Why? Dr Sharp, at least, was certain that there had been no mistake, only a delay. "I have no doubt that in God's time we shall obtain the right sites for our prayed-for advance. Until this is granted there is a great deal to be done in preparation. We all need to be prepared by a fresh outpouring of the Holy Spirit. We here are feeling increasingly the need of new power from on high; a greater devotion to Christ, more prayer revival. It may well be that this time of waiting is intended in God's purpose to bring us to our knees more than ever in repentance, confession and supplication."

For seven months they prayed and waited. Slowly and inexorably, as they prayed, the barriers were broken down and in June the Government wrote offering them the same sites, only smaller in area, that they had asked for.

Dr Stanley Smith, in England, was thrilled. "The crisis is upon us," he wrote. "Are we to advance or stay in our two stations, with two-thirds of Rwanda unevangelized? We have the necessary staff to man two new stations. The localities have been agreed to us by the Governors. It is essential for the cause of Christ in Rwanda that we go ahead and there remains only one need to be supplied, the need of funds."

Out in Rwanda, the Sharps and the Guillebauds lost no time in making the thousand-mile journey over the soft earth roads to visit and negotiate for both sites. It was the dry season and the going was less perilous. Mrs Guillebaud's car did fall through one rotten bridge, but no one was hurt and the incident is barely mentioned in their letters.

"I will send My messenger and he shall prepare the way," was the word given to Dr Sharp on this occasion. And at Shyira the population welcomed them with open arms. The crowds of sick people, who had never before seen a white doctor, kept Dr Sharp and the ladies working for hours, and Mr Guillebaud sat a little way away, reading passages of his precious newly-translated Rwanda Testament to an audience which never seemed to tire. At Kigeme there was more hostility and suspicion owing to an unfriendly chief, but plenty of people told them, privately, that they were welcome. They travelled home rejoicing. Like Caleb and Joshua long ago, they rallied their fellow workers. "Let us go up at once and possess the land."

Once again they applied, prayed and waited. On 12th October 1931, the Bible reading in the Scripture Union notes which many of the missionaries followed was from Deuteronomy 1: "Ye have dwelt long enough in this mount. Turn you, take your journey and go . . . unto all the places nigh thereunto in the plain, in the hills . . . *possess.*" As many of them were still reading, the mail man was tramping along the road from the Belgian capital, Kigali, with the bulletin in his hand: "*Vous pouvez occuper ce terrain immediatement.*"

And then a cable came from the Home Council who had that year taken over the whole financial responsibility for the Ruanda Mission, saying that owing to lack of funds, only Shyira was to be occupied.

But to the missionaries on the field it was clear that to delay the occupation of Kigeme would mean its certain loss. They were a small band, a number of them now young parents, and all denying themselves to provide for their own departments of the work. Yet, with one accord they all decided to give up one-seventh of their monthly salaries for a year, rather than lose Kigeme.

As usual, they wasted no time. Young Jim Brazier, who had been out for only a little over a year, set off from Kabale in December to live in a small, grass hut on the lonely height of Shyira hill and to hold the post until the Jacksons arrived. It was a perilous trek through the flooded valley of the Nyabarongo river and then there was the climb of three miles up a twisting road cut out from a rocky hillside, with a string of thirty porters carrying all his equipment. The nights were cold and lonely, but there was plenty to do by day. Hundreds came to help him level the first building site, and very soon about two hundred patients were coming daily to his exceedingly amateur dispensary. He was a pastor, not a doctor, but that worried nobody. On Christmas Day, after a bare fortnight's work, a hundred people gathered to hear about the birth of the Saviour.

Those were glorious, active days when there seemed no limit to the service a strong, consecrated young man could do for God! Jim Brazier was heartily sorry to leave his hill-top and his grass hut when Bert Jackson and his young wife, Frances, arrived in 1932, and the work increased with mushroom rapidity. When baby Ruth was born towards the end of the year, there was a cosy little home for her, a church building near by, and a dispensary rapidly going up. By 1933 people were beginning to ask for teachers and churches in their own villages, and the first little group of Christians had come out of heathendom and were baptized.

Muriel Barham, later married to Dr Goodchild, joined the team in 1933, and boys' and girls' schools were started. Seventy or eighty children climbed the immense hill on Sundays and classes had to be entrusted to teachers who had very little spiritual experience. The first doctor, Norman James, came out in 1934 and was married in Africa to Dr Catherine Mackinlay in September 1935. A letter, written by him about this time, reveals the problems: "No hospital, enormous numbers of men and women seeking the fold of the Church with little conception of the true meaning of Christianity, and the utter impossibility of so few teaching so many. I have thoroughly done up the dispensary and made a small minor-operating theatre combined with a room where I hope to have Bible talks. At the moment, my first in-patient is lying on the floor with a big abcess of the thigh. One longs for a ward. Perhaps we shall start building at the end of the year (but he had to wait till 1938 for his new hospital). We are drawing patients from a large area, up to two or three days' march away in all directions, so the daily teaching is, at any rate, heard by representatives of an enormous district. To what extent they absorb it is difficult to tell. Most of them have a very slow reaction time, and words take an appreciable time to sink in. But continually we have people coming to say they want an outschool, a teacher, or they want to read with us; that is, identify themselves with Protestants and be taught the way of salvation. Naturally, there are mixed motives for this."

There was some persecution from the Roman Catholics when the people turned to the Protestant religion, but there was also often a great gain for those people. It was a step out of bondage, fear, filth and ignorance into cleanliness, medical care, the thrill of education and the joyous assurance of salvation. The tremendous, uncompromising demands that Christ made on His disciples did not dawn on many at first, for there were so few who had faced them or were free to teach them. The missionaries at Shyira were deeply burdened, as they were at Kabale, Gahini and Kigeme. Ezekiel's parable was being enacted in their midst. The dry bones had come together into the form of a man, but there was little of the breath of life.

"The spiritual tone of the Christians has been low for some time," wrote one, "and things came to a head just before Christmas when Mr Jackson and Mr Verity had some talks with Christians and straightened out some troubles. Definite sins, such as stealing and drinking, were dealt with, but we realized that any lasting change can take place only by the Spirit's power." It was the heart cry of the whole band, who had sown so widely and reached such abundant outward results, yet were so deeply conscious of the shallowness of it all. "Come, oh Breath, and breathe that these may live."

Meanwhile the Mission was casting its roots on the beautiful hill-top at Kigeme. Geoffrey Holmes had acquired a wife, Ernestine, and they settled together in a small, grass house in a district far less friendly than Shyira, where the rainfall was phenomenal! "When I was at school," wrote Geoffrey Holmes, "I found it hard to understand where all the water came from that made the Nile rise so regularly. The explanation is simple. It comes from Kigeme. Our little grass house bore up bravely for a time, but after a few days we found the only way to keep dry was to put a tarpaulin over the roof." But the scenery was glorious, the countryside the most vivid green imaginable, and Ernestine was a born home-maker. "They live in the cunningest little grass house imaginable," reported Dr Stanley Smith, "and I would need to be an artist to describe the charm and cosiness with which Mrs Holmes has adorned their simple home."

They seem to have been an excellently matched couple.

Perhaps no one but Geoffrey Holmes, with his military discipline and pioneer determination could have succeeded in building a mission centre in the face of so much determined opposition. The Administrator forbade the local chiefs to sell him wood, so he went exploring, found a valley twenty miles away in the forest, and from here the trees were cut down and posts and planks carried to the Mission. His workmen feared and respected him and the building went steadily forward; first, a room for instruction and worship, then a home for the missionaries and, by 1933, the foundations of the third mission hospital. Mrs Holmes drew the women by her gentle ways and cheerful acceptance of hardship and, once again, people flocked to the mission centre. By the middle of 1932, about two hundred were gathering to the Sunday services, and people were coming from the villages three to eight miles away to ask for teachers. "Yesterday", wrote Geoffrey Holmes, "I saw on the far side of the valley a line of small figures coming in my direction, and as they got nearer I saw they were youngsters coming to the Mission for instruction. Their average age was about seven, and all but the leading file were arrayed in their birthday suits. They each carried their little elementary reading books." As usual, it was impossible to cope with the crowds, but in 1932 two brave young teachers, Filipo and Erisa, had manned outstations and were faithfully teaching growing congregations.

Kigeme was blessed in the team of African Christians who joined them from Gahini; men who had been convicted and renewed and who came to them afire with the love of Jesus. Perhaps on their arrival towards the end of 1931, they were daunted by the bleak climate and missed the warm community friendship of Gahini. They were ringed round by bitter opposition from their own people who refused even to sell them food and firewood, so they gathered on their first Sunday afternoon in an old brick shed in the valley, a fearful, discouraged little group, and they started to pray. They never doubted that converts would be given, but it was the spiritual quality of those converts that burdened them, and that afternoon God revealed to them that as they sowed, they would reap. As they laid the foundations, so the building would rise. If they were careless in their living and set a low standard, all the converts at Kigeme would follow their example and the Church would be corrupt from the start. So, down there in the brick shed, they re-dedicated themselves to complete surrender of everything that could stumble Christ's little ones.

They had come as builders and workmen, but some felt the call to remain. One, who asked leave to fetch his wife and build a hut, was warned to think it over carefully. "Do you really want to give up your home in Gahini?" he was asked. "The climate is cold, the building will soon be finished, you will be out of a job and what will you do?" "My mind is made up," he replied, "I long ago decided to live here for Jesus' sake. If I get wages, well and good, but if God wants me to be poor, I don't mind. I will live for Jesus here among the people, and try and win them for Him."

In 1933 the Stanley Smiths took over from the Holmes, and with the coming of a doctor, the medical work developed rapidly. Over the next few years patients came from the whole of Southern and Western Rwanda, and the Gospel was taught in hundreds of villages. They found a good shepherd and pastor in Nikodemo Gatozi, who had once been a coarse, brutal, government headman, till he heard the Gospel at Gahini and became a nominal Christian. But one night, while taking family prayers, he had read the verse, "Take heed, lest at any time your hearts be overcharged with surfeiting and drunkenness," and he could read no further. He went straight to the back of the house, poured out his beer and smashed his clay pipe. From that moment he became on fire for God and had been one of the first to offer for Kigeme. He was later ordained.

Under the care of these loving, simple Africans, a true group of like-minded Christians grew up and, in 1934, Jim Brazier and his wife returned from leave to help with the organization of the growing Church. The vision of a completely united, racial brotherhood had still not entirely been realized, but God was already working deeply in the hearts of the missionaries. "We are very ordinary people", wrote Dr Stanley Smith, "and misunderstandings arise and feelings get hurt. When we met for prayer we felt that, on the lines of Matthew 5: 24, it was essential that we should seek God in a spirit of unclouded fellowship, without which all prayer would be useless. The fact is, when we get wrong with our brother, everything must stop until we are right again. At least, that is what we were shown. It all depends on the spirit in which these things are done. It is useless to do it in the spirit of self-justification. The only way is for one to find out what, in oneself, has been the cause of the trouble and at all costs to put that right. I don't know if this sounds important to you, but God is showing us that it is vital."

And there at Kigeme, they continued to learn that vital, hard, simple lesson, and the hill-top became God's training school for many. In 1937, Dr and Mrs Hindley joined the team, and Dr Hindley remembers driving from Buhiga to meet Dr Stanley Smith at Ngozi. They sat in a ditch and Dr Stanley Smith "handed over Kigeme hospital"; a ceremony that consisted in the transfer of a small notebook, listing two or three items and a page of stamps.

The Hindleys were fine, able young missionaries, and the medical work flourished under Dr Hindley's leadership. Towards the end of their time at Kigeme two Africans walked a hundred miles to tell their message concerning the power of the blood of Jesus. Dr and Mrs Hindley wondered at the sadness and seriousness of their faces. It was some time before they realized that the sorrow and concern was all for them, and that broke their proud young hearts. Their last days at Kigeme were spent in rejoicing, as in true humility they got right with God

93

and with those around them and they set off to their new assignment at Shyira with a revolutionary message—but it was God's own message. "God is light and in Him is no darkness at all. . . . If we walk in the light as He is in the light, we have fellowship one with another and the blood of Jesus Christ, His Son, cleanseth us from all sin."

9

Burundi

It was in 1929 that Dr Sharp first put into words his dream of pushing southwards and establishing three centres in Burundi, but it was six years before his dream was realized. During those six years the unseen forces were moving, and a hidden work of preparation was going on. As early as 1932, a call came from a Danish Baptist Missionary Society, which had one mission centre in Burundi, to come over and help as the opportunities were overwhelming; and there were neither the funds nor the personnel to comply.

Then, in 1934, another significant thing occurred. A young convert named Abednego from Gahini, came to Dr Church one evening and asked him to pray as he had something very important to tell him. So they prayed in the quiet of the dark garden and the boy told how, a month or so before, God had called him to preach the Gospel in Burundi.

In February—the very same month—Dr Sharp surveyed Burundi and decided that they must open mission centres north, south and east, leaving the west to the Baptists. To do this successfully, he reckoned they would need suitable land for the three sites, twenty new missionaries "of the right sort" and £35,000 over the next five years. Dr Sharp tackled one problem at a time. In June 1934, he and Dr Stanley Smith, with Kosiya and Samsoni, set out to look for the sites, believing that the money and the personnel would follow. In contrast with the battle over Shyira and Kigali, they had no difficulty in obtaining two beautiful sites, Matana in the south and Buhiga in the north-east. They "happened" to meet Mwambutsa, the king of Burundi, who was most interested in their project and escorted them personally to Matana and gave the required permission. It was as easy as that! They came back to Rwanda with glowing hearts and faces, and sent home a cable, summing up the situation: "If the Lord delight in us, He will bring us into this land and give it to us."

At the end of 1934 two pioneers were chosen to cross the border with them and invade the land of promise. The first was Dr Bill Church, brother of Joe Church, who came out from Cambridge in 1931. Of his call to the mission field he wrote: "At that time, in the Christian Union, it was expected that one should go abroad as a missionary, unless there was a good reason against it. We gave no thought to the insecurity, danger, lack of pensions, etc. This was no credit to us. These things just did not enter our heads at this point." And it was well that he was so prepared, or he would never have survived the aching loneliness and disappointment of the first year in Burundi. The second pioneer was Kosiya Shalita, who had gone to Gahini in the early days with Geoffrey Holmes.

They had a wonderful send-off. A procession with seventy porters, many of whom were true evangelists, left Gahini on 27th December. Their hopes were high and their faith firm, and they crossed over the Akanyaru border river into the mysterious new kingdom, singing as they went. And the low, rolling hills re-echoed with the strains of "Jesus loves me", and "There is a Happy Land".

Dr Bill Church and Kosiya, following by car with Dr Stanley Smith, were cheered on the road by warm fellowship with three other Christian families who welcomed the Ruanda Mission with open arms: the Chilsons of the American Friends, the Haleys of the Free Methodist Mission and the Hans Emmings of the Danish Baptist Missionary Society. All truly one in aim, they held that evening, although they did not realize it, the first meeting of the Protestant Alliance that was to become

Rwanda Chief of the 1930's
(photo by the late Dr A. T. Schofield—published by permission)

Kigezi's Peacemaker. Archdeacon Ezekieri Balaba, M.B.E.
(1893–1965)

Kabale Convention 1965. Dr Joe Church speaking, with two interpreters. The words mean: Truly Jesus satisfies

Church and Congregation, Bujumbura

such a strong basis for the missionary work of the future. But that possibility was only glimpsed that night. It was enough for Dr Church that Mr Hans Emming gave them books in Kirundi, the language of Burundi, and the promise of sawn timber, and they all set out again the richer for the prayers and friendship of their fellow missionaries.

The country to which they came lacked the grandeur and majesty of the great Rwanda peaks, but it had its own beauty. The red mud roads often ran through valleys with low, vivid green hills rolling away into purple distances on each side; and cloud formations massed behind far ranges of black mountains. But the valleys are wonderful places for birds; crested eagles, crimson plumed roostmacs and long-plumed whydahs flit across the road or roost in the scrub. Buhiga hill, the final goal, slopes down the head of a forty-mile long valley where a river tumbles over the rocks in a series of waterfalls, and here on the bare hillside, Bill Church pitched his tent and started to build a grass hut, and here Dr Stanley Smith said good-bye to him and left him to it with his team of African helpers. But there were compensations and unexpected generosities. The head of the agricultural farm, five miles away, sent him a hundred trees with which to build, and Jim Brazier, no doubt remembering his own experiences on Shyira hill-top, rode down on his motor-cycle and left it as a gift to help the work.

There were many difficulties. A Roman Catholic priest took up residence on the same hill in order to warn the people against the new teaching, and rumours were rife. Bill was reported to have cannibalistic tendencies and at first the Africans would only run past his hut. He was ill with malaria and his first letters give the picture of a very lonely man. The time had not yet arrived when a missionary mixed socially with his African brethren.

"Pioneer work sounds most thrilling in England, but I find it rather damp. As I write, rain pours steadily on to my tent and in a storm I have to support it. Pioneer work means starting from scratch on an expanse of wet grass, in a congested tent. Cooking is done in an ant-hole, medical work out of soap boxes. Instead of a large number of friendly Christians, there is a crowd of pagan strangers, and thieves come nearly every night. Of society there is none, except for myriads of mosquitoes which pay nightly visits. I fear my manners will deteriorate during this year. Please don't think I'm complaining. On the contrary, I'm enjoying a new experience. I believe this is where God would have me serve Him and that is all that matters."

The medical side encouraged him, for even working from his soap box, he soon had the satisfaction of relieving appalling suffering due to ignorance and traditional practices. He remembers a woman with a retained placenta. The "midwife" had pulled so hard on the cord that the whole uterus was turned inside out and had then been smeared with cow dung. He scraped off the cow dung, pushed back the uterus and she recovered. And there was a boy carried in, blue in the face and almost lifeless, with a bean stuck in his throat. The doctor drove a knife into his wind-pipe, the boy suddenly gave a great cough and the bean shot out and nearly hit the ceiling. The boy took a deep breath and seemed none the worse. It was incidents like this that gradually won the trust and respect of the local population, and very soon he was overwhelmed by the enormous response to his message. By the end of the year there were, in addition to the Buhiga church and dispensary, five village churches and ten evangelists, and other places were asking for teachers.

But Bill Church was a realist. He was not particularly encouraged by the vast numbers. "I know what draws these hundreds of Barundi," he wrote, "it is our medicine and our money. The Barundi are much too polite to refuse anything the white man and his helpers teach. They agree to everything and love singing hymns and repeating prayers. If I asked those who wanted to follow Jesus to stand up at our Sunday service, I have no doubt that the whole four hundred would rise to their feet. Why! If I asked them to stand on their heads when praying, I believe they would do their best to please me. No, mere assent doesn't deceive us. It means little or nothing and such people will be scattered by the first real persecution that comes along. We are praying that the Barundi may begin to think about our message and show signs of spiritual life; those sure signs of conviction of sin, sorrow for sin, and a desire to conquer it. When we see a hunger for righteousness, a desire to pray, and a desire to witness to others, then we shall know that the Gospel has taken root at Buhiga."

The year was up and he did not know of one person truly "born again". The local population consisted mostly of peasants, short and stocky, and of very low intelligence, their minds set firmly on things material. But, as in other places, they were thronging into the fold of the Christian Church, and Bill, with clear-sighted humility, attributed this largely to the little group of Gahini Christians. "Their help has been invaluable," he wrote. "Not only do they help with the buildings, but they are continually teaching the Barundi, visiting them on their hills, inviting them to come to be taught. We realize very clearly, now, that the success of our work depends largely on the quality of the African Christians. If they are twice-born men, filled with the Spirit, the Barundi will take notice of their message. If, on the other hand, they are secretly thieves, drunkards, liars and adulterers, our cause is lost and we may as well go home."

He set high standards for his Christian workers, too, which was why the work progressed slowly, but on solid foundations. "It is fatally easy", he wrote, "for the African to rely on the white man for everything. . . . We feel that the evangelistic work on the hills should be paid for and run by the Africans themselves, in contrast to the evangelist supported by European funds. They will never take a real interest in it until it is. We are at the beginning at Buhiga and we want to build on sound foundations. All our ten evangelists are paid from the monthly gifts of Buhiga Christians and the money is administered by a senior Christian. The Barundi are getting hold of the idea, and have provided most of the ropes, trees and papyrus for their village churches. Pray for guidance in this tremendously important issue."

If it was hard for Bill Church to be left in a tent on the top of Buhiga hill, it was perhaps even harder for Kosiya Shalita and his small band who went on to occupy Matana, to be left alone on that piercingly cold plateau ninety miles further on to the south-west. Kosiya had left his wife and family at Gahini, and his heart ached for his little Janet and Noel and the baby. He lacked the "novelty" a white missionary offered, and at first people were merely rude and hostile. They refused to sell him food or firewood or even to work for him, and with their own hands the little group built the mud and wattle church and school. They had little knowledge of medicine and nothing to attract—except the quality of their lives and the love they demonstrated. But Kosiya had recently learned the secret of endurance and was ready for this test. He had not really been happy at Gahini, for his heart had not been entirely in the work and he had gone on holiday deciding not to return. But he visited his old school at Budo and saw, as though seeing it for the first time, the stained glass window of the Crucifixion and the words engraved underneath, "All this I did for thee. What hast thou done for Me?" "Many times at school I had cleaned that window and it meant nothing," he confessed, "but suddenly on that day it meant everything." And because it had come to mean everything, he stuck out that cold, lonely year, and found great inspiration and encouragement in the biography of Hudson Taylor. "We cannot all be Hudsons," he wrote, "we must be what we are and do what we can, and let the Lord use us as He pleases. It is not the work, but the workers and the motives that matter; but other people's lives do help us to improve."

And their lives *did* attract. By the end of the year Kosiya had
established a boys' school and several outstations, and was
teaching a number of inquirers. He was trusted and respected
by all, from the Belgian officials to the simple hut-dwellers.
Firm, lasting foundations had been laid by the time Dr and
Mrs Sharp joined him at the end of the year, with Sister Berthe
Ryf from Switzerland and a team of evangelists from Kabale.

Now things began to move. Buildings went up. Trees,
lawns and flowers were planted, which, against the vast, blue
panorama of mountains, were soon to make Matana the most
beautiful mission centre in the country. Many gifts were sent
from England for the development of the work; but the first
gift for the new hospital was given by two very small girls,
who came to the London office early in 1936, in person and
presented 3 shillings and 4 shillings respectively "for the
new Matana Hospital", and went away solemnly with two
receipts. The postal order for 7 shillings was sent out by itself,
a promise of things to come, a pledge that the £1,000 needed
would soon follow. And, sure enough, on 14th June 1937, the
Governor of Ruanda-Urundi came to Matana and performed
the opening ceremony of the new hospital.

"Dr Sharp had a tremendous gift for getting things done,"
wrote a fellow worker. "At Matana he built a hospital, a church,
schools, an evangelists' training school, and three mission
houses, in five years and with Kosiya Shalita he started about
seventy outstations over a wide area. All these places
had to be visited, chiefs contacted and maps drawn. In addition
he was building up the hospital work and was a capable,
courageous surgeon. He never seemed in a hurry." But he had
a fine team of Africans and Europeans in those first fruitful
years. Towards the end of 1939 the beautiful rose-brick church
was completed, capable of holding a thousand people, and the
great native drums installed in the tower echoed over the valley
summoning hundreds of willing worshippers.

But perhaps some of the most precious memories of Matana

centre round the Guillebauds: Harold Guillebaud, a loved figure, usually wearing an overcoat, going out for walks after tea looking like the Pied Piper, followed by wide-eyed children listening to nursery rhymes translated into their own language; teaching a newly translated hymn to any who would listen, in the quiet sunset hour when men came home from the fields.

He had returned to Africa in 1936, torn between the claims of the Rwanda Pentateuch and the New Testament for Burundi, but decided on the latter. He came to Matana and mastered Kirundi, found a workable common form to harmonize with the many dialects in use in the country and in co-operation with the Danish Mission, produced the four Gospels, several Epistles and a part of the Prayer Book. In 1937 his wife and Lindesay came out to join him before he had to leave again. The opposite pulls of family duties and his translation work must have been agony to him, but in both he gave a priceless gift to Rwanda, for Peter and his wife, Rosemary and Lindesay all came out under the Ruanda Mission. It was at Matana that Lindesay, a girl of twenty visiting her father, received her clear personal call to service, and it was at Matana that he later died, and where Rosemary finished the translation of the Kirundi Bible.

The third centre in Burundi that Dr Sharp had planned was not opened till 1936, and once again that experienced pioneer, Geoffrey Holmes, settled for a third time in a tent on a hill-top, sharing it with Graham Hyslop, an accountant recently out from England. The hill was called Buye and it was just across the valley from the government post of Ngozi. It was planned to be the headquarters of the Mission and the residence of the newly appointed archdeacon, Arthur Pitt-Pitts. It stands on a high plateau overlooking the valley that divides Rwanda and Burundi and, a hundred miles to the north, the peaks of the Bufumbira range stand out in clear weather.

The Archdeacon, in spite of delicate health, would gladly have shared the pioneer hardships, but contracted typhoid fever and it was some time before he could join the rapidly developing little colony; for there was less opposition here than in the other centres and when Lawrence Barham and his wife joined them in 1938, they found a boys' school, eleven village churches, and an overflowing congregation in the little thatched church. Julia Barham and Irene Copeland (who later married Gregory-Smith of Kabale) lost no time in starting a girls' school; and medical work was opened in 1939 with the coming of Dr and Mrs K. L. Buxton who had previously served in Ethiopia.

As at each of the beginnings, glowing reports of overwhelming numbers encouraged prayer helpers; but those on the spot recognized the dangers and cried to God for a true work of the Spirit. Dr Bill Church voiced the feeling of them all when he wrote at the end of his first year at Buhiga:

"Last Sunday we had a congregation of nearly six hundred and there is much to encourage us, but it does not blind us to the fact that we do not know of a single person who is born again, not one who has really grasped the Gospel and the meaning of it all. At our last day of prayer, Bishop Stuart of Uganda reminded us that the chief thing we were sent out to do was to convert unbelievers. We need to remind ourselves constantly of this, because it is the one thing that matters, and without it all our work must be of little value in the sight of God."

But he could not see the future, nor how many of the dirty, thieving little children clad in skins, who daily swarmed around him and his building, would grow up true, witnessing Christians. He did not know that among that very crowd of mischievous imps who so hindered his work, was the future Bishop of Burundi.

10

Life Out of Death

While new centres were being opened and the Gospel carried to the far corners of the land, the first established stations of Kabale and Gahini were going through stirring times.

The uprush of new life and love at Gahini had its roots far back, probably further back than we can possibly trace, in the prayers of saints, missionaries and martyrs long passed on. But in 1926 Dr and Mrs Norman Green stayed with the C.M.S. secretary in Kenya, the Rev Arthur Pitt-Pitts who, as we have seen, was later transferred to the Ruanda Mission as the first Archdeacon. During their short visit they were present at one of the weekly prayer meetings in his home when a small group of men and women gathered and prayed in power and faith for a great outpouring of the Holy Spirit, and covenanted to go on praying till they saw the answer. After the meeting was over, Arthur Pitt-Pitts said, "You know, Norman, God has got us to the place where we've cried out, 'Oh God, give us souls or else we'll die.' " These prayer gatherings continued till 1930 when Mr Pitt-Pitts went home to England, but by then, God's answer was becoming visible all over Rwanda and Uganda in two ways: in a deep, divine discontent in the hearts of many Christians, and a new realization of the meaning and power of prayer.

From Kabale Lawrence Barham wrote in 1931, "It has come home to us lately how desperately low the spiritual standard is here in the Kigezi district. We have been brought, one by one, to realize the state of things, and have been seeking God's face to find out where the failure lies. We believe that God has put this hunger in us because He means to satisfy it. We believe God is going to give us a big new blessing and a growing longing for the things of God."

In desperation, in 1932, an earnest attempt was made to cleanse and deal with the moral problems of the Church. Notorious sinners, after being pleaded with in vain, were publicly excommunicated and the offenders escorted off the church precincts, but the effort, though sincere, achieved little. First, it concentrated attention on one or two glaring sins, such as adultery and drunkenness, and passed over such hidden sins as pride, jealousy and secret theft. Certain fruits were cut off, but the root remained untouched. Secondly, time had yet to show how fallible and mistaken the missionaries often were in their judgments, how blind to see and how slow to believe what evil still lurked in their "special" converts. Not till the Holy Spirit caused every man to judge himself could there be any real cleansing.

No, the revival did not come through human effort; it came through this widespread hunger and thirst for God and His blessing, that brought men to their knees and made them fulfil God's conditions, however costly. In the spring of 1932 Joe Church was in England, pleading with the student bodies to pray, and one day he spent time praying with Paget Wilkes of Japan. This saint and warrior exerted a profound influence on him, for Paget's views on a holy life were uncompromising and his aim clear and simple. "The greatest need of the heathen world", he was fond of quoting, "is my own personal holiness."

Then, in September 1933, the first mission conference was held in the beautiful setting of Lake Bwama. The Rev A. St John Thorpe and the Rev Arthur Pitt-Pitts were the speakers and it threatened to be a time of deep controversy. Opinion was strongly divided over the advisability of introducing the full paraphernalia of the Church of England into the infant Churches of Africa; and also as to what part the non-ordained layman might play in the Church.

Feeling ran high and the usual Bible readings and prayer meetings seemed a mockery. Only a man of the spiritual stature of Arthur Pitt-Pitts could have coped with the situation. He cancelled the original programme, and a whole morning was spent seeking to get right with each other in a spirit of humility; and many a zealous missionary who had come determined to stand up for his or her principles at all costs, discovered how much of that so-called "principle" was rooted in pride, obstinacy and jealousy, and how love and reason had been wrecked on these hidden reefs. Prayer took the place of argument and the issues were settled without personal offence and resentment. "I think God asked us one question very searchingly at the Convention," wrote Dr Stanley Smith. "Are you a praying Mission? And in the true sense of the word, we had to say 'No'. That is to say, prayer has not been our most trusted resource; it's been an extra, a help on occasions, but not really the most essential means by which we could put ourselves in God's hands to do His work in the hearts of men. I believe we can say it is not the same now. God is doing a new work among us. Please pray that it may deepen and grow till God can, without anxiety, entrust us with the fullness of His power."

"Prayer is either a force or a farce," wrote Joe Church. "I believe that in some mysterious way only revealed to us in the life to come, prayer is the material means by which our bodies can be tuned into God and become channels of His power to flow through to man. We can work furiously, learn languages, organize and build, but all will be as chaff if we are not tuned in. Prayer is an attitude of mind, not of body. We must be living in communion with God every moment of the day. To kneel at a prayer meeting may be as ritualistic as turning a rosary. 'Could ye not watch with Me one hour?' The disciples were asleep because the burden of prayer had not yet descended upon them. They had not yet seen the Cross."

Back at Gahini the burden of prayer was coming down on them, longed for, yet bitterly contested. The team consisted of Pat Walker, Yosiya Kinuka and Joe Church in the hospital. Dora Skipper was leading the women's work. Captain Holmes had the oversight of the churches and Blasio was in charge of the evangelists' training school. With such strong and varied personalities, unity and harmony were hard to achieve. The extreme irregularities in ward work caused by revived African staff rushing off to testify in their homes, and the complete disruption of school timetables caused by meetings prolonged hours over schedule, were a breath of life to Joe but chaos and confusion to Pat Walker and Dora Skipper, and even worse to the military Mr Holmes.

But in the end, grace and humility triumphed and something new and very precious emerged that was to be one of the foundation-stones of the revival. Two reconciled missionaries asked forgiveness of their African brethren, to the amazement of the latter. "Never before have we heard a white man own that he was wrong," they said wonderingly to each other, and united prayer was easier after that; and it was about this time that the idea of "teams of two" started.

Lawrence Barham came on a visit to Gahini, developed chicken-pox and stayed ten days. His bedroom became a sanctuary for him and Joe, as they entered into a deep, lasting fellowship of prayer and claimed revival. "If two of you shall agree . . . it shall be done"—and truly, it was being done all around them as the yearning to pray spread. By 4 a.m. on Christmas morning 1933, the dark verandah outside Joe's house was thronged with men who could not sleep because they must pray, and they went on pleading with God together until the mists rose, the sunrise gleamed silver on Lake Muhazi, and crowds began pouring in from outlying kraals and villages to rejoice because Christ was born.

Life Out of Death

The conference for African evangelists and teachers that started on 27th December was, to begin with, no different from the usual conference: good orthodox teaching, good attention and many rather impersonal prayers. But some expected something different, and so sure were they that some further blessing would be given that they invited their guests to stay for an extra day of special prayer.

It was 3 p.m. on that extra day and nearly time for the congregation to start for their scattered homes. Man after man rose to pray formal, correct prayers on the missionary pattern; prayers that seemed to rise no further than the roof and to reveal nothing of the true inward need of the one who prayed. To Kosiya Shalita the atmosphere was deadly, stifling, defeated, and he slipped outside under the open heavens and cried out in desperation to God. And, even as he cried, a man in the church stood up and, instead of offering up the expected list of petitions, he started to weep and confess his sin.

The Spirit had come amongst them. For two-and-a-half hours men rose, sometimes several at a time, overcome by conviction of sin. There was uncontrolled weeping and crying out, followed by overwhelming joy and burning love. One after another offered to carry the news of the Saviour's redemption to the farthest parts of the land. It had suddenly become so glorious, so sweet, that they simply could not keep silent. One by one they set out, to the extreme disruption of school and hospital routine and the intense annoyance of some of the more orderly minded. Truly they "went out with joy and were led forth in peace", while to their newly opened eyes the high mountains of Rwanda seemed to break into singing before them, and the trees in the valleys clapped their hands.

At Gahini the Spirit continued to work and the opposition continued to grow, but in the midst of the conflict men increasingly began to be conscious of one dominant, Spirit-filled figure who stood as a rock in the storm, Blasio Kigozi. Paget Wilkes' words could have been written of him at this time.

"Men turn again and again to the few who have mastered the spiritual secret, whose lives are hid with Christ in God. They are of the old time religion, hung to the nails of the Cross."

Blasio was the younger brother of Simeoni Nsibambi, and had been brought up by him in Kampala. Simeoni spent hours teaching the boy and praying for him and at last led him to the Lord, "My first-fruit in Jesus," as he called him. Blasio's first idea had been to join the legendary evangelist Apolo in the pygmy forests of the Congo. This proved impossible owing to political factors, but he had been unable to settle down or accept any of the good teaching posts offered to him because he knew there was a call for him to go somewhere beyond the distant border of Uganda, whose purple horizon he could see from the top of Namirembe hill. So, in 1929, when the appeal came from Gahini for a master to come and build up the boys' school, Blasio immediately volunteered. So sure was his call that he told Simeoni that he was prepared never to come back to his native land of Uganda, if necessary, but to lay down his life in Rwanda that her people might be saved.

He had arrived in Gahini in 1929 at a critical time and worked hard with Cecil Verity. In 1932 he went back to Uganda to study for ordination and in 1934, the year when the Spirit of God had begun to move in a new way, Blasio was welcomed back as an ordained deacon. He became close friends with Yosiya Kinuka and opened the evangelists' training school in January 1935, to face a very difficult first term. The seventy young evangelists were apathetic and resentful of Blasio's zeal and in April, after hours of "hearing words", six packed their belongings, put their bundles on their heads and walked out, leaving Blasio overcome with a sense of failure and inadequacy. In a way he had never done before, he cast himself on God crying out, like Jacob, "I will not let Thee go except Thou bless me."

Some time before, he had built a little round prayer hut with room for two, himself and the Lord, and he now retired into this hut and stayed there for a week, seldom appearing, and eating very little. Few people knew what was happening, but during that week he received the power he prayed for, and he returned to his work the same pleasant, cheery Blasio, but with a difference. There was a new zeal, a new sense of urgency, a new freedom and assurance and he spoke and wrote openly of the experience he had passed through. The following extracts from a letter sent to Lawrence Barham were typical of many written at that time:

"We have had some trouble like you have been having at Kabale and this caused six boys to go away for good. This trouble caused me to think deeply about my life, and I have found that I am not right with God, and it has become a burden to my mind. I therefore straightway laid all the sins that God manifested to me at Jesus' feet, and I am writing to tell you about this. They were not very big sins, and some I hardly noticed. At the same time I was troubled about the Christians' Bible class as I seemed to see not a single person whose life was changed, although I was running it for three months. For these two things I earnestly prayed and now we have had the blessing, and mine came to me on the day of Pentecost. Now the whole atmosphere has absolutely changed. To my bed, where I lay for two weeks, three boys came and openly confessed their sins, and now there are more than a dozen born again. These have changed the tone of the whole school. Nowadays they come to me as their friend and consult me in their troubles. It is a joy I have never experienced since I first began to work for Christ.

"For the last two months I have been fighting the flesh. It keeps asserting itself and wants to master my soul as it had done for many years past, and sometimes I am defeated. I am peering into the distance and seeing that Christ is coming towards me to crucify it. He is facing me, but sometimes I look away. I wish He would punish it because it is pride. Pray for me in my weakness and in my deeper striving for spiritual experience."

Blasio was fearless in his preaching of sin and repentance and many resented his direct condemnation of their faults. But he radiated love and the spirit of Jesus and wherever he went men were convicted of sin and drawn to the Saviour. From Gahini to the outlying districts the flame of revival spread, and on to Kabale, as a team led by Blasio travelled up north to tell of the great things God had done for them. The detailed events of this journey will be dealt with in a later chapter, while we continue to trace the personal story of Blasio.

The young schoolmaster, Joe Church and Yosiya Kinuka had developed a friendship and spiritual unity probably hitherto unknown between black and white. They spent hours together praying and studying their Bibles and it was about this time when the words of a motto card, hung on Joe's wall, seemed to burn themselves into Blasio's heart.

I'll preach as though I ne'er will preach again,
A dying man as unto dying men.

He was often found gazing up at those words, and during the closing months of 1935 he was gripped with a new sense of urgency, as a man who knows his hours are numbered. He seemed to be burning himself out and everyone was glad that his holiday was nearly due. He had planned to go home to Kampala. His devoted wife, Catherine, and baby James had left before Christmas expecting him to join them in about three weeks' time.

Then followed a strange, swift-moving drama. On 19th December, Joe Church travelled up to Mbarara in Uganda to get Christmas stores, expecting to be back in a couple of days' time. But the car broke down and spare parts were unavailable, so on Christmas Eve Joe found himself pacing up and down the long avenue of eucalyptus trees that led to the cathedral, feeling bitterly disappointed and resentful. Away in Gahini, Decie,

John, David and baby Robin, would be spending Christmas
without him, and he would miss the glorious celebration of
Christ's birth in company with his dear Africans, whom
Christ's spiritual coming had filled with such joy and love and
power. The orthodox atmosphere of the C.M.S. Mission at
Mbarara, with its conventional services, was repugnant to him
and he had not failed to show it. He had been asked to preach
at the Christmas service, but he knew that many were critical
of what had happened in Gahini and Kabale, and he was
miserable.

But there, under the eucalyptus trees, Someone seemed to
speak to him. Just three words: "If ye abide." They checked
his rebellion and self-pity and steadied him. He apologized to
Mr Clarke, the missionary in charge, and Mr Clarke, who was
a brave, understanding man, made a bold move. Just before
Joe was due to preach, he came over to him and whispered,
"May I announce that you will hold a mission here in three
weeks' time?" Joe immediately said, "Yes."

Two days later Joe was back in Gahini, putting the invitation
to Blasio and Yosiya. To him it was a wonderful new opening
from God, but Blasio hesitated. He was exhausted and perhaps
no one realized how he had counted on his holiday. Catherine
and baby James were waiting so eagerly in the home back in
Kampala. He stood considering, until suddenly Yosiya broke
the silence with these strange, prophetic words, "Blasio, this
may be the very last work God has given you to do. Do we
know when we shall die?"

This decided him, and a fortnight later Blasio, Yosiya and
Paulo from Shyira set off northwards. It was an utterly new
departure in Uganda for Africans to be teaching missionaries,
and Mr Clarke had taken an important forward step in inviting them. Glimpses of what happened are best told in Blasio's
own words in these extracts from long letters he wrote to
Dr Church.

"It was God's plan for us to come to Mbarara. There are lots of signs. It is all God's plan and God's will. Pray and pray. Last night I was very much convicted about the state of the perishing and the deadness of the Mbarara people until I couldn't keep myself from crying, so we are putting into our programme the subject "kurimbuka" (to perish). Lots of these people are simply asleep. They are perishing, but they do not know it.

"God has guided me in my quiet time that we must all three speak every time. It does not matter how long we are, *if people are saved*. So we start today with all three of us, each taking thirty minutes and a hymn before each talk.

"12th January 1936. We have come to the last day of the mission. I am writing this from where Yosiya is staying, with a man *whose life is saved*. Praise God! Praise God! I wrote to you about our programme which included destruction. Yosiya says he has never lived closer to Christ than he has this week. Paulo has wonderfully grown.

"Tonight all the teachers came and people were invited to witness to Christ. One man was unable to stop himself from crying and there were about six others. Tell our praying friends they have shared with us, and all of us have shared with Christ. We had no time to sleep at all the whole night, visiting two homes.

"Pray unceasingly for me. I'm going to face some hard problems regarding my three points for Buganda clergy."

So the mission ended and the three friends travelled to Kampala on the back of a lorry at the usual breakneck speed, singing hymns and praising God, but there was not only a holiday ahead of Blasio. He had already sent on a paper to be read at the Synod of the Uganda Church, boldly denouncing deadness and materialism, and pleading for repentance. In it he included his "three points", the result of months of pondering, grieving and praying.

On reaching Kampala he joined the retreat for clergy, to be held before the Synod began, and although he was only a deacon, the Bishop asked him to address the gathering. Fearless and uncompromising, he besought these clergy to make sure that they were really born again; to be more diligent in saving souls rather than in collecting money. Some resented it; some were impressed by his obvious sincerity. The Synod promised to be an exciting time!

But he never reached the Synod. While still at the retreat, he was taken ill and carried to Mengo Hospital, where his temperature rushed up to 105° F, probably from tick fever contracted in one of those small, unhealthy homes where he had sat talking all night. Yosiya, his brother Simeoni, and his wife Catherine, stayed beside him nearly all the time, quietly praying and singing hymns, except when he insisted that Simeoni should go and tell the other inmates of the ward about Christ. He knew he was going to die, and gave explicit directions. "I want to be buried outside the cathedral," he said, "so that those coming from Rwanda, when they stand to rest, may look at my grave and remember where I was buried, but there must be no tears for me."

He died on the evening of 25th January and the Bishop, who had visited him frequently during his short illness, conducted the burial service in the great cathedral on Namirembe hill. His grave lies near those of Mackay, Hannington, Pilkington and others who brought light to Uganda, and a vast crowd attended the funeral. But his brave voice spoke on, and a great hush fell over the Synod when his three points were offered for consideration:

1. What is the cause of the coldness and deadness of the Uganda Church?
2. The communion service is being abused by those who are known to be living in sin and yet are allowed to partake. What should be done to remedy this weakness?
3. What must be done to bring revival to the Church of Uganda?

Life Out of Death

Blasio's suggestions were these:

That complacency in the leaders, together with loss of urgency and vision in their teaching, were the causes of the coldness and deadness.

That revival could only come by the way of new birth, the coming of the Spirit, and the claiming of His power.

At Gahini the news was received in stunned silence. Their leader was gone; the one from whose Spirit-filled preaching and faith and prayer the revival had seemed to spring. But this was God's way. The man was taken home, and the Spirit that had worked through him seemed now, in a new way, to be working unconfined; a wind blowing where it listeth. Strange things began to happen in places where there had been no human activity at all. There was no longer any human leader. The Spirit Himself was in control, and all over the land men turned, not to a Spirit-filled man, but to God Himself.

11

The Sound of a Mighty Wind

"It is useless to try and organize a revival," wrote Edwin Orr; and certainly complete lack of organization and total opposition to all preconceived missionary methods and theories seem to have marked that wave of blessing which swept through East Africa in the thirties. So much so that it was a time of deep conflict and controversy because pet theories and preconceived ideas have deep roots and are not easily shaken.

It started at Gahini in Blasio's lifetime, and spread to Kabale. After his death it spread like a forest fire all over Uganda and Rwanda, uniting, dividing; wounding, healing; bringing peace and a sword; breaking down and building up. Human effort and direction seem to have had little to do with it, but the wave of prayer that went up from many parts of the world as a result of Joe Church's pamphlet, *Victorious Praying*, no doubt had much to do with it. Here it is, in full:

VICTORIOUS PRAYING
A Plea for Revival Prayer Fellowship

THE NEED IS URGENT

Behind the apparent success of Christian missionary work in Central Africa, those who know have seen that "life had become stagnant" and they have wondered, "what power can make the dead bones live?"

We are now witnessing God's remedy for man's backsliding.

The Sound of a Mighty Wind

The Holy Spirit has come in power and is making dead bones live. From 1933 a movement of Revival has started in the Ruanda Mission, and God is calling out bands of consecrated men and women in many places far beyond the borders of Rwanda. These people, once lifeless and formal Christians, though leaders in the Church, have passed through deep conviction of sin and have emerged absolutely changed men.

From among these, bands of men and women have gone out as "Bible Teams", fired with a longing to bring this new life to others. In every place they have visited they have left behind groups of people bound together in a deep prayer fellowship. They have a vision of the fire of Revival spreading right through Central Africa to our own home country.

The object of this leaflet is to link up this prayer fellowship, growing up in widely separated places and in different nations, and to mobilize prayer for this Revival at home among those who know the power of prayer. We send this out with a sense of urgency. It is one of the tides of God's Spirit "to be taken at the flood".

God has shown us quite clearly that the conditions for the granting of His blessing to this fellowship have been the common bond of absolute surrender to Christ. And the only praying that is certain of results is that of those who know this same secret.

So we ask you, who will join in upholding these Bible teams, to seek as you pray to find this same blessing through a heart that has become a cleansed channel. God will send Revival through your prayer if He has first revived you. That prayer so used in China is coming to our Africans: "Lord, bring Revival and begin it in me."

THE WAY TO VICTORY

To us European missionaries, this Revival has been a searching experience and most humbling. Time and again we have found that it is we who have hindered God's blessing. We have had to be humbled to the dust. So it is not superfluous for us all, as we pledge ourselves to pray for this Revival, to see again the Way to Victory.

The secret of all true Revival, and the fellowship that knows no barriers of race or class or privilege, is personal unbroken communion with Christ.

McConkey says: "It must be simple. God would not have made it difficult. It is we who have made it ambiguous by our doctrines theories, theologies. We take refuge in prayer . . . pleading . . . social service . . . giving our wealth. Thus we dodge the real issue, which is absolute surrender to Him who was received at conversion. It may be years or at a single bound, but every saint of God knows that this crisis must be passed. . . . The Devil will fight for the last stronghold of the soul. . . . God states His condition of blessing: there is no other."

One cannot organize a Revival; it is mysterious as the wind. All human attempts at working up Revival are mere emotionalism—are man-made fire. Even the organization of prayer can be mechanical; there is an invisible bond that unites the hearts of men who are truly on fire.

We need to remember that this Spirit-filled life is the will of God for everyone of us, and that anything less than full surrender is sin. It is sin to be lukewarm. It is sin to fear, for fear is either pride or doubting God. A self-centred life is sin. The smallest compromise on moral standards is sin. And sin separates. If we are to abide in the place of power and blessing we must, with instant and continual obedience from the heart, yield these sins to the cleansing victory of Christ.

Once right with God as far as we know, we can enter by grace this place of Revival immediately. We do not have to wait for God: He is waiting for us. And the secret of continuing here is constant obedience. We cannot live on the merits of a past obedience. But perhaps we have for years been living un-surrendered lives, and a mass of hidden sins have been allowed to creep in and clog the life: and so we have grown cold and ineffectual in the service of the Master.

AM I LIVING THE VICTORIOUS LIFE?

May we suggest, as a practical daily test when we meet with our Lord, we ask ourselves a few questions, and so daily renew our vows. People sometimes "sign the pledge"—why should not we sign a pledge against the subtler sins of hypocrisy, pride, jealousy and malicious gossiping? When we deliberately hand over these things to Christ we experience immediate victory. The Lord Jesus remains the same yesterday, today and for ever. The Victorious Life is free to every Christian, and no sin or human failing is unknown to Christ or barred from the list.

Let us ask ourselves then about some of the things to which we have become "addicted". They can still lead us to "squander our living" and they can even lead us into that very real prison, "bondage to self".

QUESTIONS

(a) Am I experiencing defeat along any line in my life, such as jealousy, impure thoughts, fear, hypocrisy, mistrust? Am I running away from life? (Malachi 3: 3)

(b) Have I an uneasy conscience or any unforgiven wrongs? If so, the remedy is simple, and there is only one. "Leave your gift at the very altar and go away; first be reconciled to thy brother" (Matthew 5: 23, 24; Moffatt).

(c) Am I doubting God? Doubt and unbelief are perhaps the worst sins of Christians. We say to God: "You can't change me"; "I'm made that way"; "I can't love so-and-so". This is the I-dolatry of believers, and is in reality doubting the Holy Ghost. But the Cross is "I" *crossed out* (Mark 6: 5, 6; Hebrews 3: 12).

(d) Have I fallen into spiritual pride by saying: "Lord, I thank Thee that I am not like so-and-so," or have I acquired

119

that subtle superiority complex towards men of other nations and colour?

(e) Do I grumble and complain? Remember Moses' words: "Your murmurings are not against us, but against the Lord" (Exodus 16: 18). Oswald Chambers says: "If we give way to the *luxury of self-pity* . . . we banish God's riches from our own life, and hinder others entering into His provision . . . self-pity puts self-interest on the throne." Augustine prayed: "Lord, save me from self-vindication."

"The receiving of the Holy Spirit is God's answer to repentance and faith.

"The fulness of the Holy Spirit is God's answer to surrender and faith" (McConkey).

So many stop short at repentance and acts of re-surrender. They lose sight of the basis of it all which is real faith, that is, the staking of *all Life is and all it holds* on the One who "is able also to save them to the uttermost that come unto God by Him, seeing He ever liveth to make intercession for them". Many have spent years praying, whereas God was all the time waiting for them: "All day long I have stretched forth My hands unto a disobedient and gainsaying people." Do not let us blame God.

REVIVAL IS COMING, IF——!

Here, then, in simple obedience to Him lies the secret of blessing, and here only can real Revival Prayer be prayed and mountains be moved. That is why we stress it now. . . . How miraculous is the result of this praying!

Revival is like an African bush-fire: as it burns and spreads over the mountainside all that lurks in the long grass, the snakes and the rats, have to flee for their lives.

Revival is like the storm of long-expected rain which comes at the end of the dry season and brings life again from the dusty veldt. But before the reviving rain falls, black clouds will appear and trees will bow and fall before the wind.

The Sound of a Mighty Wind

Revival is like a delicate and beautiful flower that can only thrive and bloom in prepared soil. The soil is the surrendered heart, and the garden looks upward to the sun. But all "roots of bitterness" must be daily weeded out.

Revival is the fruit of the Spirit, and is, therefore, normal spiritual life. God's command is: "Be filled with the Spirit" (Ephesians 5: 18), and God's promise is: "I am come that they might have life, and that they might have it more abundantly" (John 10: 10). We must never blame God if we have not the fullest peace and joy in this life. He is holding it out to us to take, if only we have faith to do so. It is not by works. "Works belong to the workshop. Fruits belong to the garden."

As we face these things it may mean for us an entirely new surrender of our lives to Christ. This may be a humiliating experience, accompanied as it is bound to be by restitution and reconciliation, but there is no other way and no short cut to Revival.

"Men ablaze are invincible. Satan trembles when he sees the weakest saint upon his knees. Fire cannot compromise. Sin, worldliness, unbelief, hell, are proof against everything but Fire. The Church is powerless without the Fire of the Holy Spirit. Destitute of Fire, nothing else counts: possessing Fire, nothing else really matters. The one vital need is Fire" (Samuel Chadwick).

And so we ask you in Jesus' name to take up the burden of prayer for Revival, and to enter into this invisible bond of fellowship with the bands of men and women who, fired with a new life, are carrying the flame of Revival into these Central African kingdoms. Effectual praying might bring about a mighty movement of God's Spirit from Congo to Kenya and throughout the whole world.

Let this prayer, well known, but so searching, be ours daily:

"Lord, bring Revival and begin it in ME.
For Jesus Christ's sake. Amen."

J. E. C.

The Sound of a Mighty Wind

This pamphlet was published in May 1936 and in September Archdeacon Pitt-Pitts wrote, "There is a deep relationship between this movement and your prayers. I have been to all the centres where this revival is going on, and they all have the same story to tell. The fire was alight in all of them before the middle of June, but during that last week in June, it burst into a wild flame which, like the African grass fires before the wind, cannot be put out. And as the story is told by Miss Skipper at Gahini, or Miss Forbes at Shyira, or Mr Barham at Kabale, the same dates stand out. One asks the reason why, and the answer is found in that large crowd of praying people, who have read that call to prayer that was written by Dr Church and the appeal that people should pray for the Mission which was being held at Mukono just then. So often we in the mission field send home an S.O.S. asking for prayer, but I think we forget to tell you the result, and still more often leave out the matter of praise. I would ask that those who read this letter should try and make time to join us in thanking the Master for what He has done. It should be a great encouragement to prayer to know that this thing has not happened by accident, and when you pray, God does hear and answer."

This upsurge of new spiritual life had started in Kabale in 1935, when a young hospital dresser from Gahini, aflame with the joy of forgiveness and the love of Christ, had begged for a week's holiday to go and testify to his friends in Kabale and in the Kigezi district. Lawrence Barham and the Rev Ezekieri Balaba had been praying for years for God's breath of life on the dead, formal Church at Kabale, and in this young dresser they saw that spirit of praise and testimony so lacking at their own mission centre. The letter from Blasio, previously quoted, confirmed them in deciding to write to Gahini and to ask for a team of Christians to visit them.

The team arrived in October to hold a ten days' convention for the three hundred teachers and evangelists scattered over the Kigezi district. But even before they arrived, those who had anguished in prayer for so long had seen the break. They were not only a few now. The hunger for blessing was so great that men in every department began to meet for prayer. "And as we prayed," they wrote, "we seemed to get strength."

The team was led by Blasio, Yosiya and Joe Church, but they all felt that Simeoni Nsibambi, at Kampala, was meant to be with them, and Joe wrote asking him to come. But God had already told him that he was to come and spend a month in prayer in the Bufumbira mountains and preach to the leprosy patients at Bwama, right there near Kabale—and he had saved part of his fare for this long journey. So he arrived rejoicing and the convention started with two quiet days of prayer and the chorus: "Spirit of the living God, Fall afresh on me," was sung over and over again. The scheme followed the one that had been used at Gahini, pursuing a different subject each day; sin, repentance, the new birth, separation, the victorious life, the Holy Spirit. And during these meetings men were convicted of sin, and trusted "Christian" leaders confessed that they had never been born again at all. Sums of money, stolen years before, were returned and a great longing was born in those who loved the Lord to go out all over the district and tell others about Him.

It was a heart-searching, yet joyful, time, but it was not till those same teachers and evangelists had gone home to their scattered congregations amongst the banana patches that the real results of that convention began to be seen, and strange reports began to come in from little country churches of Kigezi. Through those teachers, now born again, cleansed from sin, and consecrated to God, Christ Himself reached out to the people. Men, women and children flocked to the churches many brought there by dreams. Whole congregations would cry out and tremble before God and pray all night. Many would fall to the ground in paroxysms of grief and remorse as they saw their sins; and numerous stories are told of that time. Great was the joy in the little church when a man of evil repute stood up and recounted how he had been told in a dream to look up the number of a certain hymn and sing it. He woke and got up at once and found that the hymn was:

> *I lay my sins on Jesus,*
> *The spotless Lamb of God.*

and as he sang, he turned to the Saviour.

A girl who had twice been refused baptism had flounced angrily out of the girls' school saying, "I'm off to the Roman Catholics. They'll baptize me." Now she came back and handed to her teacher at the door a sheet of paper on which was written "Please forgive me. Jesus Christ has." On being invited in, she said, "I was very, very angry and refused to read my Bible or pray, but a voice kept saying in my heart, 'It is you who are bad.' I said, 'No. It is my teacher,' and I argued for a long time with that voice, but in the end I went to my hut and found my New Testament. It was dirty and the rats had eaten part of it, but I read it and prayed, 'Oh Jesus, forgive me the anger that crucified Thee.' Then I fell asleep, and the next day I knew that you had been right and I had been wrong, and until I had met Christ that night, I had never been converted. I had always been an angry girl, but I stopped being angry, yet the roots were still in my heart, and I had to let Christ dig out those roots. He has done it now, and He hurt me, but I am glad."

One old woman tried to speak several times, but each time she was overcome with emotion. At last she managed to tell how, during the famine ten years before, she had killed her small grandchild because there was no food for him.

Little children rose to their feet too. "I know you will think it strange for a little girl to stand up," said one, "but Jesus loves little children and I know what a sinner I've been and now I want to love Him and live for Him."

Yet the tide of blessing brought its own complications of hysterical imitation, criticism and division, and Lawrence Barham and Ezekieri Balaba had a hard time counselling and teaching, all over the district, on various problems. One group, for instance, were sure that the Lord was returning at once, and wanted to know whether or not they should plant their crops.

Back at Gahini, Blasio's death had acted as a trumpet call. Even before he died, at Kampala a senior lay-reader called Ezera, had dreamed that he was swimming in a river and Blasio, in a boat, was drawing him along with a rope. When Blasio died, Ezera felt sure that he should go straight to Gahini and carry on Blasio's work, so the position of school-master was quickly filled. Many said that Blasio's death had made them decide on a new life of witness and seeking for power, and the head builder returned twenty francs he had stolen, and told publicly how he had lived in sin for years. Dr Church's letters, written at that time, give vivid pictures of what was happening. "Several times Christians from various departments have gathered on Saturday nights, and three times we have prayed till midnight for power and zeal. Last Monday the term ended with a day of praise, and from 9 a.m. until 1 p.m. we sat and listened to testimonials of new life, inter-spersed with hymns, from the seventy evangelists. One, especi-ally, was remarkable. A moving confession of past failure was given, and then an old, dirty native gourd was produced, full of water. Sin had made his heart like that, but now he was broken. He smashed the gourd on the cement floor and returned to his place and prayed."

The outward manifestations of revival became progressively more violent, and in the summer of 1936 many missionaries felt there was real cause for concern. One night, at the girls' school, about six Christian girls went off to a classroom to pray and as they prayed, one after another joined them until nearly the whole school was present. A tremendous sense of sin gripped the company; three or four prayed at a time and many wept and cried out until they collapsed on the floor. Confessions were sobbed out far into the night, and the resump-tion of normal classes was impossible for days, as girl after girl asked leave to go home and pay debts or restore stolen property.

In the church the same thing was happening. There was loud weeping, rolling on the floor and trembling, as men cried out their confession of sin, and their manifestations of joy when they experienced God's forgiveness were equally alarming from the European point of view. Drums were beaten and men danced and swayed outside the church like pagans. So great was their relief that they sometimes went on singing hymns all night, to the annoyance of weary missionaries who were trying to sleep.

In July, Archdeacon Pitt-Pitts came to Gahini and preached to a congregation of a thousand. Such was the weeping and trembling that it was impossible to finish and only after many hours did he persuade all to leave, except for about two hundred who appeared to be under deep conviction of sin. Deeply concerned, he and Mr Verity warned the leaders against the dangers of hyper-emotionalism and Miss Skipper, fresh from her experiences in the girls' school, was perplexed and afraid. But the Africans would have none of it. Weeping and shaking are signs of the work of the Spirit, they maintained, and if you do not do it, you cannot be filled.

At Kigeme, Jim Brazier and Dr Stanley Smith prayed and waited, and began to see a stirring of conscience and a confession of sin among the evangelists. Then a woman evangelist arrived from Gahini, and the same outward manifestations of the working of the Spirit began to appear. People began meeting to pray at all hours of the day and night and that same overwhelming conviction of sin descended on them, but those two experienced missionaries seem to have been less alarmed than most. "Some of us were frightened because of the violence of their conviction," wrote Jim Brazier, "but its proof is in the results. Those who have had these experiences are changed, new creatures indeed. In fact, most of them have had such a vision of the doom to which their sins were bringing them that they have been in a state of hysteria, bordering on unconsciousness. I have talked with many of them and their vision has remained with them, every incident real, every word plain. There has followed such a flood of confession and restitution that it is difficult to control it if, indeed, it should be controlled. And it is not confession for the sake of the praise of men, for it has brought many to shame and disgrace. We have seen the outer covering stripped, and hearts as they really are, desperately wicked and incurably sick. It has been a shock to us as well."

The blessing spread abroad all round Kigeme and, in 1937, Miss Lanham told of the wave of blessing that had reached the hospital itself. "Only one of our hospital boys cared at all," she wrote, "and he was on fire. But in January God began His work and two of the junior boys were saved and others became very restless and miserable. Then about two weeks ago the trained midwife and another senior boy were marvellously convicted and converted. How, why, when or where, I cannot tell you, but both are now bursting with joy."

In most cases, as the fierce, almost hysterical emotion passed, there arose something from the dust and ashes that no missionary could gainsay; a love and zeal that glowed and burned and must testify. More and more bands went out and Joe Church, at Archdeacon Pitt-Pitt's suggestion, was relieved of medical duties and set free to organize the sending out of the teams, often accompanying them, and wherever they went they carried their Saviour with them and crowds flocked to hear His voice. "A wave of spiritual blessing seems to be spreading through the Mission," wrote Archdeacon Pitt-Pitts. "Numbers are not everything, but I want you to see in these great crowds Christ standing. They are looking at Him and He waits to express Himself to them through His servants." In the summer of 1936, the Good News was carried from Kabale in the north, to Matana three hundred miles south, from Buhiga in the east, to Kirinda in the west by Gahini evangelists, who wished to spend their holidays preaching Christ. Esiteri, a high-class Tutsi widow, walked two hundred and fifty miles from Gahini to Buhiga, via Kigeme and as she passed the Spirit worked.

A team revisited Mbarara, that respectable stronghold of Anglicanism where Blasio had wept and prevailed. Here they preached again, and a Christian government official suddenly fell on the floor, weeping and howling. Incoherent with grief, he told them he had seen Christ looking out over the lost, grieving for their awful condition. Others, too, sat weeping, saying surely Christ had come to the church, for they, too, had seen Him.

At Mukono, Blasio's bold, written message, only read after his death, hung unanswered in the air. It was here that the Christian leaders of the Church were trained, and it was this place that Blasio had felt to be the key of the whole situation: conventional, orthodox, theologically sound, governed by the rules of the Church and the Mission. But the Spirit of Life had not, as yet, breathed through it and the Bishop knew it. With great daring he asked Joe Church and Lawrence Barham to bring a team of Africans from Rwanda, and for the first time Africans, missionaries and Bishop were housed under one roof and enjoyed a quiet week-end in fellowship together.

And then prayer was answered, the prayers of thousands who had just received the newly-published *Victorious Praying*. The tense, critical atmosphere of the meetings, the veiled sneering, gave place to awe and weeping. These were no ignorant Africans speaking, puppets on a platform, pushed forward above their station by new-fangled missionaries; these were men of God. About forty "nominal" Christians found Christ for the first time, and Sunday ended with a mighty meeting of praise, epitomized by one who could only throw up his arms and cry, "Jesus, you are a wonderful, wonderful Saviour to me."

At Kako, in the great bat-infested church, the usual respectable congregation collected and the place was shaken. One convert sold his shop at once and went off to preach revival in distant Tanzania. At Bweranyangi they were joined by a young man, whose voice was later to be heard all over the world, William Nagenda; the young pastor there was Erica Sabiti, who was to become Archbishop of the Church of Uganda, Rwanda and Burundi. Here extraordinary happenings took place. Anderea the cattle driver was at a heathen wedding one night when a girl cried out in terror, "Look! There is fire on the backs of the cattle!" A great fear came upon him, and an urge to go to the dark church to pray. He resisted, but the Voice would not let him rest. At last, trembling, he climbed the hill to find that the church glowed with a soft light. About thirty others had heard the Voice and had come, weeping, through the darkness to seek God.

Samsoni, too, felt that strange fear in the night and put out his hand to take hold of his charms, but Someone gripped his hand and a Voice said, "Take these to Sabiti." Terrified, he called his wife and they set out at once, only to be joined by a girl who ran out from a house near by crying, "I, too, want to burn my charms." A well-known drunkard was enjoying himself as usual when the Voice spoke. "Why do you mock me?" it said, and he rose up trembling and poured his calabashes of beer out on the ground, and hurried off to the meeting.

Over the border into Burundi went the evangelists, and at Buhiga a notable witch-doctor was converted, publicly laid out his bones, coins and rubbish, and told the awestruck crowd that the charms were worthless, and he had now found Jesus Christ. Stolen goods were restored and sin was confessed. From Matana Dr Sharp wrote, "At the usual Sunday morning service on the thirteenth of June, many came under deep conviction of sin and about sixty stayed on to an after-meeting. One by one confessed aloud to God and sought His mercy. We had the great joy of explaining the way of salvation, and hearing one after another accept Christ and praise Him for forgiveness and salvation."

On the mountain-top at Shyira in Rwanda Dr and Mrs Norman James and Berthe Ryf prayed and waited for the wind of God to reach them, and again it came with visitors from Gahini, radiant with what they had seen and heard. So, there at Shyira they stopped all work for two days and people met to talk about sin, repentance and salvation. On the second day conviction of sin came to some. One trusted Christian worker after another confessed to anger, pride, stealing and adultery. One handed over the price of an injection he had not paid for, another the cost of a hymn-book. One happy lad remarked, "My! The new birth is a wonderful thing! When I went into that meeting I had no intention of getting up, but the Holy Spirit spoke to me. When I saw Mrs James sitting near me, I thought I could never confess to stealing her sugar, so I just sat and held my head in my hands until I couldn't sit any longer. I nearly fell through the floor when I stood up and confessed my sin."

Later the Hindleys came to Shyira rejoicing in the new blessing that had come to them at Kigeme. After a period of resistance and opposition, one after another came to the light and let their veneer of respectability and hypocrisy fall. The headmaster and his wife and senior teacher, the senior hospital worker and the acting pastor, all confessed to living in secret sin for years. The wife of an evangelist held up a torch and said, "Last night God met me. His Holy Spirit shone in my heart as I shine this torch on my friend, showing me what is in my evil heart."

The leprosy settlement was not passed by. In 1936 a team from Gahini visited Bwama Island and a patient from Kigeme, called Simeoni, was deeply moved. He had worked as a nurse in the hospital and was a prey to terrible fears; fear of death because he was not saved, fear of life because of the progress of his disease. But, to tell the story in his words, "That day

I was pierced in my heart and more afraid than ever. A Voice said, 'Repent,' but Satan also spoke. 'Repent, but don't give up sinning. Put those medicines down the drain but don't confess.' 'Shall I have peace if I do this?' I asked myself, and I asked my wife to give me advice. 'Don't steal any more,' she said, 'but don't confess.'

"But I found no peace, nor could I any more look into people's faces because of the darkness of my sin. Then one day I could bear it no longer and I brought it out to the light and confessed. There was no other way. Friends said, 'He is mad,' but I have found peace." Shortly after this, two more were converted and the four of them became a team to pray for the others. The others resented it and persecuted and falsely accused them. Life was hard and bleak and one evening two of them—just before the sunset, when the lake to each side lies level and golden—entered the cool, dim church and began to sing and pray. Perhaps they were weary of their diseased, ostracized life; perhaps Simeoni was thinking of the four little daughters buried by the shores of Bunyoni; in any case, they sang over and over again the hymn with the refrain:

> *In the sweet bye and bye*
> *We shall meet on that beautiful shore.*

and, as they sang, one patient after another crept into the darkening church to sing with them—the lame, the blind and the disfigured, rejoicing at the prospect of meeting on another shore. Soon the building was full and they sang and prayed until morning, and on and on, while the sun travelled up the sky. Hospital work was apparently forgotten (one can understand why harassed, overworked Sisters were not always completely in favour of the revival). Dr Symonds came over from Kabale to do the ward round and wondered where his staff was, but he, too, joined the great congregation and they sang on until they had no voices.

"I ached from being hugged," went on Simeoni, telling the

story thirty years later. "On the third day many, many people repented and were saved. My wife was saved, too. I stopped worrying about my illness" (here his delight overcame him and he jigged gently up and down in his chair and hugged himself). "Slowly I got better and I prayed for a hospital for leprosy patients in my own country."

God heard his prayer and later he went to the first leprosarium in Burundi, where for twelve years he worked as a male nurse and led many to Christ. In 1961 he was discharged and came to be the trusted senior worker at Kigeme Hospital. His face lights up as he tells his story. "Because I was ill, I found Christ. I was in despair like Jonah in the belly of the whale. He brought me up; he lifted me out."

Evelyn Longley wrote of many at that time bringing back clothes and blankets and all sorts of stolen goods; but perhaps the chief sign of the revival was the new radiance and courage that shone out on ravaged faces, the new sense of the near presence of Jesus in their pain and weakness. One old man insisted on living on in his own hut long after he should have been in hospital and the nurse pleaded with him. "I worry about you all alone at night," she said.

"I am never alone," replied the old man. "When those chaps go away and shut the door at night, Jesus comes in and stays with me. When they come back and open it in the morning, Jesus goes out. . . ." So, day by day, he waited for the evening when his Lord would come in to stay with him.

12

The God of the Valleys

It was a time of joy and a time of sorrow; a time of conflict
and a time of reconciliation; a time of wounding and a time
of healing—and no hearts were more torn and perplexed
and bowed down than those of the missionaries themselves.
Some rejoiced, some feared, some openly opposed what was
happening. They were often divided from the Africans and,
even more often, deeply divided among themselves, and it is
well to look back over this stormy passage of rough water and
try to understand what caused such divisions and even, in
some cases, such bitterness and estrangement.

First, one must consider the background of these missionaries. For all their faith, courage and deep devotion to
Christ, they were products of their age, and their age was that
of post-war colonialism. The slogan that was paraded in
Uganda when Edward, Prince of Wales, visited them, "Tell
your daddy we are happy under his rule," was probably not
coined by the Africans. It was the naïve belief of colonists that
any people over whom the British flag waved were to be envied
their privileges; and in a sense they were right. The British had
brought with them education, a medical service and increased
prosperity, and their houseboys were well treated provided
they knew their place. And, because the rural African loves a
quiet life and is a clever fellow, he usually conformed exactly
to the colonial conception in public, while quietly carrying on
his own unchanged private life behind the scenes. Very few
whites knew anything about the real person behind the obedi-

ent, servile façade, and most of the missionaries were no exception, loving and devoted but unconsciously patronizing, seeing
themselves, because as yet no other vision had been given them,
as white, beneficent chiefs among simple Africans who humbly
accepted all they had to give, including the Gospel.

They were also products of their class. Most of them in the
twenties and early thirties were from what would, in those
days, have been termed the upper middle class. Their men
were usually reared at public schools and universities, where
all manifestation of enthusiasm was tabooed and all excess was
considered to be bad form; where self-control and understatement were the tenets of a rigid code and to break this code was
to lose caste. If emotion must be spilled, it must be done in the
inviolable privacy of one's room.

> *Though I am beaten,*
> *Nobody shall guess,*
> *For I will walk*
> *As though I knew success.*

That was the sentiment to which they would most heartily have
subscribed.

But God had a different vision. He wanted to show the
world a new conception of fellowship that would override caste,
code, background, race, colour and prejudice. It was the only
real answer in the world to war, hatred, racial superiority and
apartheid; and perhaps He chose this group of missionaries
through which to display this vision because with all their inherent pride, rigidity and unconscious reservations, they loved
Him and desired to know and do His will.

Perhaps the first hurdle that had to be faced was Joe Church's
insistence on an equal brotherhood of Black and White, and
that Colossians 3: 11, pushed to its logical conclusion, was the
only possible basis upon which a self-governed, self-supporting
indigenous church could grow. But the germ idea caused consternation. It cut at the very roots of convention and threatened

to dissolve the whole social pattern. Some missionaries prophesied no good at all from Mrs Guillebaud's habit of allowing
the Africans to crowd into her house for Sunday hymn singing,
or Joe Church's custom of letting them sit in his room as
equals and share news from his letters. Even when those
African leaders grew in spiritual stature and were being used
of God in East Africa as no missionary had been used, they
were only accepted with caution and sometimes not at all. Mr
Clarke dared public opinion when he invited Blasio's team to
lead the Mbarara mission, but he *could* not—no, please, he
could not—invite them to lodge and eat in a European home!
So they were sent to three small African homes, and Blasio
wrote about it with characteristic meekness. "We are not all
staying at the same place; we are spread out all over Mbarara.
We wanted to pray together hard, but God planned differently.
We tried to sleep in one place, but God did not wish it."

It was Bishop Stuart at Kampala who first invited the whole
team to his home for a quiet week-end before the Mukono
convention, and demonstrated publicly to the Christian communion in Uganda that brotherhood on equal terms was both
safe and desirable.

Another important step forward was in Kenya, that stronghold of colonialism when, in 1937, missionaries and African
pastors first sat on a convention platform together and ad-
dressed a mixed company, a new idea bitterly opposed by
some. But the idea took root and it proved its point that
brotherhood in Christ meant indeed a new relationship. And
there in Kenya the fellowship that transcended race and colour
became the one and only solution to the horrors of the
later Mau-Mau rebellion and the only loyalty that could hold
men together. "Through the experience of this persecution",
wrote one who was there at the time, "there is growing up in
Kenya a new conception of fellowship; fellowship between
African and African; fellowship between African and European; and it is upon this fellowship that the future of Kenya

largely depends. The way of fellowship is the only hope for Kenya, but it is costly. It has cost the blood of martyrs, the precious Blood of the Son of God Himself, and it is not only Kenya that is involved in that cost, for the way of fellowship is the only way for the world." So gradually Christians learnt the truth of what Dr Aggrey, the great African in the Gold Coast, wrote, "You can play some sort of a tune on the white notes of a piano, or on the black notes, but to produce real harmony, you must play with both black and white keys."

Then there was the question of excessive emotion: the shouting, the dancing, the hysterical manifestations, so utterly repugnant to the English gentleman and soldier, so completely suitable for those only recently emerging from paganism, who knew of no other way of expressing overwhelming grief or extreme joy. Many who had prayed earnestly for revival were horrified when it came. It is easy to see—after a lapse of years —how much it was a matter of temperament, how foolish it was of the Africans to insist that there could be no real work of the Spirit apart from crying and trembling; how unwise of missionaries to try so hard to check what resulted in such joy and praise. But it was not easy to assess true values in the very heat of the battle, and certain missionaries simply could not endure it and left the mission field. There was the awful "irregularities", too. Of a busy hospital morning the Sister wrote, "The senior dresser has gone off to testify and the doctor is all over the place!" It did nothing to pour oil on the troubled waters, either, when the doctor in question told her that spiritual blessing must come before timetables and rules, and she must be careful not to keep back blessing.

At the school in Kabale too, things got out of hand. "These revivals are all right," wrote the teacher in charge, "but when you get an ignorant people who can, and do, work themselves into such frantic states, I feel we are not doing right to leave them unguided in such matters as singing hymns far into the night and attending prayer-meetings at all times. One teacher, in charge of the school dining-room, just came into meals and then went straight off to sing and pray. You can imagine the state of the dining-room, but when I remonstrated with her she replied, 'I have no eyes for the things of this world; I see only the things of God.' This sort of thing is happening many times a day and I have decided not to have the two ringleaders back after the holidays." So they were told there was no room for them, an action strongly criticized by the other missionaries.

But there was no doubt that those who had passed through the emotional stage came out with a radiance and spiritual strength that left the tired, perplexed missionary right in the shade. Some of these missionaries, too, were deeply humiliated by the awful disclosures and confessions that had been made by their trusted workers, about whom they had written so glowingly in their prayer letters, when all the time there had been nothing but hypocrisy and deceit. What did Harold Guillebaud feel when his dear fellow-worker in the Bible translation suddenly stood up and produced all the paraphernalia of witchcraft? What did any of them feel when one trusted church leader after another admitted to consistent immorality, stealing and drunkenness? What had all their years of work and prayer amounted to? Apparently nothing.

And then, harder still to bear, these same "converts" in their simplicity, and in the light of their new, glowing standards, began to turn on these very missionaries who had led them to Christ and taught them, and to accuse them of coldness, lack of zeal or—in extreme cases—of not being born again at all. It was the last straw. One can well imagine the emotions engendered according to temperament: the wounded pride and resentment, the attempts to justify, the humiliation and the crippling sense of failure, the final temptation to despair, to give it all up and go home.

Wounded by the Africans, often estranged from their fellow-missionaries because there were extreme left and right wings and every degree of opinion between, to whom could they turn but to Christ Himself? They had worked so hard and sacrificed so much. They had yet to see that "a broken, contrite spirit" was the last sacrifice God now required of them. One by one, they began to do exactly what the Africans had done, only with less outward commotion. They began to accept the criticisms, confess their sin, lay it on Jesus and enter into a peace and fellowship they had never known before. The old façade of superiority and race distinction had been pierced through and discarded; they need never pretend any more.

And on the other side, those who had been critical and hard had to learn tolerance, charity and humility. Dr Adeney writes, "I remember how we missionaries at Buhiga, after the steadying, wise influence of Bert Jackson had been taken away, tried to purify the Church. No one who was not revived, we decided, could preach any more. A leader who we thought was not right with the Lord was excluded from our meetings till he repented. What coldness came over the place that had been so full of praise! Eventually things got so unhappy that we sent for Lawrence Barham from Buye, and we all met in our home, none excluded. A little snake came in and we killed it with a stick, but it provided a wonderful text for Lawrence's message. It had lifted its head and tried to resist, just as we were fighting and justifying ourselves. The Lord had taken Psalm 22 to Himself, and there He says, 'I am a worm and no man,' and worms don't resist. How the Lord used this message to melt us and, with real sorrow, we asked forgiveness of the one we had excluded. From then we were able to go on in new love for each other."

"Three evangelists came to Buhiga," wrote a devoted pioneer doctor, "and during a conversation with me they stated that, in their opinion, I was not born again. Indeed I was still in the way of destruction. To my surprise, four of our leading Christians at Buhiga supported them. They gave several reasons for this opinion, among others, that I had never confessed my sins in public with tears, and did not know the meaning of a broken heart. I thought they had confused sanctification and salvation, but it became clear that they meant exactly what they said. As they insisted in this opinion, I sent for the Archdeacon who, after a good deal of thought and prayer, revealed to them their mistake. . . . God has been teaching me many lessons through this humiliating experience. Pray that I may learn all that He wishes to teach me."

"The trouble usually starts this way, I think," wrote Bert Jackson. "A young convert experiences such violent reactions from his old, heathen ideas that he is inclined to see wrong everywhere. Especially does he look for it in us and, to our shame, he often finds it. Then he says, 'How can a child of God do the works of Satan?' and a hard condemning attitude becomes the hallmark of a strong, fearless Christian. It has not been easy for the missionary to be told that he is not even a child of God, and to find that any teaching he may try to give is ignored, but we are proving at Buhiga that a quiet, unruffled spirit always wins in the end. I feel any criticism, even that made by a young, inexperienced Christian, should cause us to get low before God and ask to be shown if there is anything in it. If, after careful searching in all sincerity, the peace of God remains, then why get so rattled?"

"It has been a deeply humbling experience," wrote Dr Stanley Smith, "to be shown something of the poverty of one's service. Men and women recently born again are, some of them, those whom we looked upon as our brightest trophies and wrote of them in *Ruanda Notes*. Yet from their own confession, they were stealing, drinking and committing all manner of sin unknown to us. One just cries out, with Isaiah, 'My leanness, my leanness.' But this sense of unworthiness is no morbid thing. It has been one of the most emancipating experiences of one's life, for it has brought deliverance from the bondage of pride and, on the evidence of John 16: 8, one questions whether there can be any true work of the Spirit without this deep sense of personal unworthiness. I believe this is God's normal way of working. I can't help feeling that God leaves us to carry on in our ineffective energy, unable to help us because we think we must run it all ourselves. Then in His own time, He comes and pushes us puny creatures aside and works, and we say, 'How extraordinary,' but I believe this is His normal way of working when unhampered by our unbelief. I believe we are near the end of our troubles, but don't pray that things will settle down. We never want to go back to the old complacency. Pray the fire doesn't go out."

It was Dr Stanley Smith, perhaps more than any other at this time, who stood in the gap interpreting one side to the other, wise, gentle and tolerant. And then in 1938, when the difficulties and divisions were at their height, the harassed missionaries met for a conference at Gisenyi, the government post on Lake Kivu in North-west Rwanda. Nearly five thousand feet above sea-level the lake lies; sixty miles long, with the banks rising to forest-covered mountains eight to nine thousand feet high. The waters are clear and peaceful, but the conference tended to be a stormy one. "God showed us something of what full surrender means," wrote Dr Symonds, "and we learnt that it was not an easy thing to be broken, and He requires this of us every day. We realized, too, more than ever before, the possibilities of a life of real fellowship with each other and with the Africans. There is no doubt that many of them are farther along the line, in this way, than we are. In their sight we are no longer 'The Great White Man' but they long to walk with us and to grow with us."

"It is hard for you to realize it in complacent England," wrote Bill Church, "but we know now, that God has been chastening us and refining us in the fires of revival. There was breaking and then rejoicing such as we have never known before. Though some feared it, we followed the lead of the Africans at Buye, and devoted a whole day to the subject 'Hindrances to Revival'. There were many broken testimonies and then our fears blew to the winds and peace and fellowship came. Not one life was left untouched."

The God of the Valleys

The missionaries went back to their work humbled and rejoicing, and ready to face the problems in a new spirit; *in* the movement, instead of *outside* it as critical onlookers. One by one, young and old, they came down off their pedestals of pride, superiority and criticism, and took their place humbly in the ranks of those who desired to walk together. Many are the happy testimonies of those and subsequent years, from men and women who found a peace they had never known before in dropping all strivings and pretences, accepting criticism and facing reality; beginning at last to know because they were willing to be known.

Peter Guillebaud writes, "When I went to Africa I had heard of revival and welcomed it, even though I had received a letter from my fiancée criticizing it. I felt sure the revival must be, basically, the need of the Church. However, when I got there, married and settled down, I soon became very critical. The African brethren were too downright and the light was bright. There was plenty to criticize, of course, and I argued with them, Bible in hand, that their interpretation of the Scriptures— 1 John especially—was incorrect. I was later to see that the real roots of my critical attitude lay: (1) in my unwillingness to let the Lord show me sin in my own life, especially pride and self will; and (2) in colour prejudice. I was most indignant at what I regarded as forwardness in these African brethren.

"I blush with shame as I look back at my brashness and pride as a young missionary, and the way I argued with other missionaries old enough to be my father, who walked with the Lord in a way I knew nothing about. But worse than this, I remember with shame my haughty attitude to dear African saints; and with gratitude, their patience and at the same time, their strictness with me. I remember one car journey with Yosiya Kinuka, to whom I owe so much. I had been arguing fiercely with him, quoting the Scriptures freely, but in a proud, know-all spirit. Finally he said to me sadly, 'Some of you missionaries know your Bibles so well, but you are like a man with

141

a crate of ammunition but no gun. Someone with one round and a gun with which to fire it can do more damage."

"Gradually the Lord dealt with me, bringing me back to the Cross, and showing me that the way to go on with Jesus is the way you begin at the Cross. Colossians 2: 6 spoke to me, 'As ye received Christ, so walk in Him.' It is a lesson I still have to keep re-learning."

Elisabeth Guillebaud writes, "People ask, 'Did you join the revival movement?' And the answer is, 'No.' We went for a holiday in Uganda and there, through the witness of young revival leaders, God showed us our pride. We had come as sinners to the Cross when first converted, but had grown up away from it and become proud in our Bible knowledge, missionary training and Christian maturity. We were broken down before God and shown that we had to come back to the Cross and keep coming there as sinners. When we got back to Buye we found ourselves in fellowship with others blessed by the revival. It was as easy as that. When we got right with God we were one with these people. There were still things we did not like, but we could now share these things in fellowship together; not as critics looking at things from the outside."

Miss Skipper at Gahini had steered the school through very troubled waters and she wrote, "Last June there was a great outpouring of the Holy Spirit and that light brought a conviction of sin which was a revelation to all of us, as we have never before really been able to see into the minds of the African women. Now, the whole outlook has changed and there has been a completely new relationship between Africans and Europeans. Before we were two different tribes. The Europeans were superior people who could not sin. The Holy Spirit has forged a real bond in Christ Jesus which can never, now, be broken. There is nothing now, except sin and an evil conscience which will keep any African from telling us what he or she feels in his heart about us, for our welfare."

The God of the Valleys

"Humanly speaking," wrote Miss Langston, "I do thank faithful Africans for being absolutely honest with us Europeans, but above all, I thank God that He opened my eyes to see myself in the light of the Cross. The accusation brought against us was that we were cold—a hard crack, but a crack which meant final breaking, as it was true. On the surface everything appeared so satisfactory. Underneath, where was the life? Deep down, lives were not born again, and after a disturbed night, I saw in a new way how fruitless had been the past when I had tried so hard to do everything to God's Glory instead of letting Him do it all through me."

"During my holiday", wrote the Rev Gordon Bulman, "I became more and more conscious of how I had failed the Lord Jesus. At the Limuru conference in Kenya, there was a certain meeting where I found out a little of what Job meant when he spoke of being 'shaken to pieces and broken asunder'. I can't remember what the speaker said, but I began to say like Job, 'Mine eye seeth Thee; wherefore I abhor myself and repent in dust and ashes.' It was amazing to get back to Shyira and to find that Dr and Mrs Hindley of Kigeme and Hilda Langston had undergone a similar experience about the same time."

One new and lasting development to emerge from these difficult years was the fellowship meeting. At almost every mission centre since then there are round, thatched huts called prayer huts where, once a week, those who love the Lord, black and white, meet without reticence to testify. Sin is confessed, praise is unitedly given for victory and forgiveness. Messages from the Bible and testimonies of God's help are shared. These simple meetings, still being held, have been of tremendous value in guarding the fellowship and keeping the group together. After every testimony, those present break spontaneously into their well-worn refrain, sung softly in parts:

Glory, glory, Hallelujah,
Glory, glory to the Lamb.

Oh, the cleansing Blood has reached me,
Glory, glory to the Lamb.

"They are not special people," wrote one who observed it all. "They are just part of a great crowd of witnesses to what the Lord is doing, scattered over East Africa; ordinary folk, doing their work to the Glory of God. We are apt to build a phantom picture of revival. If we do this, revival never comes because people are looking at the workers instead of looking at Jesus. True revival is coming back to the Lord and being released from sin and finding a new joy in the home. This is lasting; excitements are not. Outward signs—weeping and falling down, dreaming dreams—accompany certain kinds of revival, but they are transitory. Jesus is God's gift to mankind and God has nothing else to give. He is revival. God can never give anything beyond what He has given in Christ. Jesus is the centre of it all."

13

The War Years

God's timing is perfect. By 1939, when the Mission had to enter the dark, difficult war years, the travail and birth pangs of the revival were mostly over and a Church had emerged, purified and tried, and ready to meet the increased demands and added responsibility about to be asked of it. Critics had said that the Mission had expanded much too rapidly, beyond its capacity to maintain and staff its work. Humanly speaking, this was true. The war years checked its advance and it had time to consolidate and cast deeper, firmer roots.

God had prepared the Mission for what lay ahead by a serious financial crisis early in 1939. The expansion in Burundi five years before had been made possible by a gift of £30,000 paid annually in sums of £6,000 and it was hoped that, by the end of five years, the Mission's usual income would be adequate to maintain the work which had begun. But it was not, and in 1939, the last year of the special gift, the whole of the Mission's finances had to be reviewed and expenditure drastically cut. In view of the existence of a new government dispensary near-by, it was decided to close Kabale Hospital, and several missionaries for whom there was no support were asked to retire. It all seemed like tragedy at the time, but a few months later when war broke out the leaders thanked God that preliminary action had already been taken, and they were at least on a firm financial basis before meeting a new crisis; for it seemed at first as though supplies from England would be completely cut off and plans were made for living off the land. All boarding schools had to become self-supporting as to food and clothes, and all pay and grants were reduced by 20 per cent for Africans and Europeans alike, and all building suspended.

Nothing but the Spirit of Jesus, imparted in His fullness through the process of revival, could have prepared the Africans for this new emergency. Nothing so forcibly proved the reality of what they had undergone as the way they reacted. Almost without exception, they accepted the cuts in their meagre pay without a murmur, and many greeted the news with joy and praise. "Satan thinks he can make us poor," said one young hospital dresser eagerly, "but he can't! We have Christ now, and so we are rich."

"What can separate us from the love of Christ?" challenged the teacher at Buhiga. "If there is no pay?" "No," replied his congregation. "If the English leave us?" "No." "If Hitler comes and burns our churches?" "No." "Why?" "Because Christ's Spirit dwells in our hearts."

Financially, the prospect in Rwanda was certainly bleak, as money in the bank in Uganda could no longer be taken over into non-British territory and the rate of exchange dropped alarmingly. But the Danish Mission set a fine example by immediately becoming entirely self-supporting and living off the land. Once it was being done somewhere, it was not so hard to believe that it could be done everywhere and courage and faith soared. At Gahini, they decided to close twenty-two churches, but sleepy members suddenly woke up and promised to undertake the evangelists' pay themselves. In almost every other place the evangelist himself flatly refused to leave his flock and carried on without pay. At Kabale, there was a united refusal to close the Evangelists' Training School, and the Africans worked out a scheme for complete self-support. At Buye, the local church took over the finances of two of the five outlying districts, and at Shyira the masters gave up their own wages in order to carry on the school. At Matana, a conference was held where, in addition to Bible teaching, they discussed plans to make the work self-supporting, so that in spite of the war there should be no retreat, but rather steady progress in the spread of the Gospel.

They worked as they had never worked before. Missionaries, Africans, men, women and children, went out into the fields and hoed together, while hymns resounded through the banana patches. At Kigeme, Joy Gerson explained to her school that they would either have to look after themselves and their teachers or stop learning, and they chose to carry on. The day-girls brought firewood and water daily, and the teachers gave up a day a week to digging and planting. All cultivated together from 6 a.m. to 10 a.m. and school started at 11 a.m. Instead of Mr Brazier employing paid carriers on his long treks to visit scattered village churches, the readers themselves would come and fetch him and carry all the loads for nothing.

They were happy, if sometimes anxious days, and many are the stories of supplies arriving "just in time". Mrs Brazier was expecting fourteen European guests on their journey south and there was very little to eat. But just before they arrived, the local chief sent round a dozen men with a little help—320 eggs, 14 chickens, 2 rabbits, 2 cwt. of peas and 80 pounds of potatoes. At Buye, Canon Barham, checking their church accounts to see if there was enough to pay their teachers, found he was 120 shillings short. That same day, letters came from two friends who said they felt that the Mission would be short of money and so they had both doubled their usual gift of 30 shillings and enclosed a cheque totalling 120 shillings exactly. The stories could be multiplied many times over.

The missionaries themselves did all they could, and their own voluntary gifts to the work amounted to £950 in the first year. Many Africans, from their reduced incomes, added another tithe; but even so they could not have carried on without some funds from Britain and these were forthcoming in a wonderful way. The initial embargo on the export of English money was removed by the deliberate policy of the British Government, to assist the work of foreign missions. "I am myself quite clear that the support of foreign missionary work in time of war is an essential part of the Church's witness; a permanent and universal Christian obligation," wrote Lord Halifax in August 1940, at the height of the Battle of Britain.

On looking back it seems clear that this financial crisis proved a tremendous blessing in the Church; a forward step from dependence on the Mission to independent maturity. "It impresses me immensely to think of the marvellous forethought of the Lord," wrote Dr Stanley Smith. "I'm quite certain that, but for the revival, this crisis would have meant disaster; but the Lord gave the spiritual blessing before He allowed the material testing and it has found the main body of the Church firmly established on the Rock of Ages. Nothing could have so surely taught them to lean in entire reliance on the Lord."

The second factor that seemed a tragedy and yet resulted in blessing, was the withdrawal of a number of missionaries from the field for financial reasons. But sprouting trees need room to grow and expand and there were men in the African Church at this point who were now capable of taking full responsibility and leadership, and they needed room in which to exercise it. The permanent departure from the mission field between 1938 and 1940 of such men as Cecil Verity, Captain Holmes and "Pip" Tribe, and the temporary departure of others, as well as a number of able women teachers and nurses, left many areas leaderless and spiritually orphaned, but God was preparing other leaders and already the scarcity of missionaries was bringing out powers hitherto dormant. Jim Brazier wrote, "The Church is in a position like that of an African with grown-up sons. Nine years ago I, the parent, did everything. I chose every church site, supervised building, inspected crops, settled disputes, received the collection. Now I have young men to do all these jobs, and one of them, Nikodemu, was elected deacon in the spring, and no doubt others will follow."

But there were two greater bereavements during the war years; places were left empty that, it seemed, could never be filled. On 22nd March 1940, Archdeacon Pitt-Pitts was called home to God.

He had first come out to Uganda in 1916 as chaplain to Bishop Willis: long, lean, gaunt, rather delicate, a typical Cambridge Christian graduate, immaculate in dress, perfect in his manners. Sir Albert Cook wrote of him, "Usually it is some time before a young missionary counts for much on the mission field, but though Pitt-Pitts had no special gift for languages, and indeed, at that time confined his ministrations to the English, we all felt within the first month that a new spiritual force of the first magnitude had arrived." Ten years later he was appointed secretary of the C.M.S. in Kenya. There, amidst much that was nominal and lukewarm, he prayed and agonized for revival. "I don't know that I have ever known a man so absolutely on fire," wrote another. "Some men flare up with rare enthusiasm and then die down, but he was always on fire. There was a spiritual power in him, which was clearly the result of a deep and continued communion with his Lord. The flame was like that of the burning bush." In 1935, in a wonderful way, he was permitted to see the answer to his own prayer, for the C.M.S. released him to serve as Archdeacon to the Ruanda Mission, where for five years he directed, counselled and advised. Compassionate, sane and Christ-like, "Pips" became one of the great shepherds of the revival with his deep spiritual discernment of the true and the false, and his quiet dependence on prayer as a stronger force than action.

He had been suffering for months from arthritis, although carrying on his work without complaint while undergoing treatment. In January 1940, he carried through the first meeting of the Diocesan Council, under the chairmanship of the Bishop, but he was already a very sick man when he set out with the

Goodchilds for a holiday in Kenya. Taken ill on the journey, he was admitted to a nursing home in Nairobi, where acute complications set in. Dr Theo Goodchild stayed with him and marvelled at the calm assurance with which he faced death, for he seemed quite sure that he was going and made all arrangements; laying down one responsibility after another, and witnessing to those who ministered to him. His only worry seemed to be that he was upsetting the Goodchilds' holiday, and he, who had so loved the Cross of Christ, died on Good Friday morning.

The ranks closed, but a terrible sense of loss hung over the whole Mission, which lifted slightly when Harold Guillebaud, who had arrived out that same year with his wife and two daughters to carry on his translation work, was inducted as the second Archdeacon in Namirembe Cathedral, Kampala. His son, Peter, had arrived at the end of 1939 to be married to Elisabeth Sutherland, who was already teaching in Burundi.

The Archdeacon travelled down to his headquarters at Buye, and wherever he went a tremendous welcome awaited him, for it was he who had given the gift of God's Word in their own language to the people of Rwanda and Burundi. But he never really recovered from a severe attack of bronchitis he had undergone in Kampala, and to his great disappointment, the weeks passed and he was unable to take up his task. He was not well enough to be present at the first ordination service for clergy trained at Buye Theological College, although it was he who had translated the order of service. He read the service to himself in bed while the others were in the church, and had the three new clergymen to tea afterwards. It was, perhaps, the biggest disappointment of his life, but his only comment was, "Shall we receive good at the hand of God and shall we not also receive evil?"

It was soon recognized that he needed skilful nursing, so he was taken to Matana, into the care of Dr Sharp, Drs Harold and

Isobel Adeney, and Sister Marion Lloyd, where he seemed to rally. It was a happy, peaceful time, and on Sunday, 6th April 1941 Kosiya Shalita conducted a little communion service for the Archdeacon, his wife, Peter, Elisabeth, Rosemary and Lindesay. However, there was no doubt that he was getting weaker and Dr Sharp and Dr Stanley Smith both felt that he should be taken to Kampala as soon as he could stand the journey.

But he did not want to go to Kampala and he never became any stronger. He asked for prayer to be offered in his room, and afterwards, the little group joined to pray with Kosiya and all the Christians at Matana. With the vision of that unfinished Bible before them, and of the thousands hungering and thirsting for the Word of God, they claimed complete healing in the name of Jesus, for the work's sake. But God had other ways of looking after His work and He answered their prayer fully two days later. "He asked life of Thee and Thou gavest it, even length of days for ever and ever."

On the morning of his last day on earth, the Archdeacon and Mrs Guillebaud were reading Amy Carmichael's *Gold by Moonlight* together. As she laid down the book, he said, "Now I know what will be my message if ever I have to preach a farewell sermon here. It is the keynote of this book that, when we can least of all understand God's ways, then is the time to accept His Will as perfect. In acceptance lies peace."

He died very suddenly from heart failure that same evening, just thirteen months after his predecessor. The funeral service in Matana Church, conducted by Canon Barham and Kosiya, was attended by Africans and Europeans from a radius of a hundred miles around. He had given them God's Word, but the task lay unfinished. "We can only remember the Saviour's words, 'What I do thou knowest not now, but thou shalt know hereafter,' " wrote Dr Stanley Smith. "The immediate result is that the translation of the Kirundi New Testament is held up, and all the Missions in Burundi are crying out for it. Pray that his mantle may fall on someone especially equipped for this vital work."

Dr Stanley Smith himself was already pressing on with the Rwanda Old Testament, and was it prophetic insight that made him turn to Rosemary as they left the grave? Rosemary, the eldest daughter, had been her father's special friend and helper all the way through, and had been called in as a child to share his joy when he completed the New Testament for Rwanda. "Perhaps God will call you to carry on his work, Rosemary," said Dr Stanley Smith, and the girl, who from the age of fifteen had planned to work with her father, wasted no time. Day after day she went to the hospital where Stefano, her father's co-translator was lying ill. By the time he was well enough to leave, she had already translated the first twelve chapters of the Acts.

God was providing new workers. To the depleted medical ranks He sent the Adeneys, and to supply the urgent need for higher educational standards in the schools He sent Peter and Elisabeth Guillebaud. Both these families were privately supported apart from Mission funds, and the Hindleys elected to come back without any regular support at all, trusting in God alone. For the spiritual leadership of the Church, new voices were already beginning to be heard from the ranks of the Africans that would later echo in countries all over the world. People were starting to recognize the power of God in William Nagenda, and in 1941 Festo Kivengere became a Christian.

The story of his conversion is best told in his own words. "I was born in a pagan home and herded cattle, but when I was nine an African evangelist started a little village church and I learned to read. One day they gave me the Gospel of Luke to take home and I was very excited and impressed. I felt a kind of attractive power in the One I read about and I knew He was a living person. At eleven I was baptized and went to a school in the north of Kigezi. There was a Scripture Union branch in the school and I was very enthusiastic, but I had no personal knowledge of Jesus. Four years later, when I was still a schoolboy, a team from Gahini came to our school and preached on judgment and sin. Something new happened. The things we had known for years suddenly became real. It was no longer a question of what Jesus did long ago. We were confronted with a living Christ, and judgment and sin became a reality and we had to do something about it. Many were convicted, but we were not converted. For the first time I saw two boys stand up and confess and make restitution. Nothing new was preached. It was the old, old message, but the Holy Spirit made it real.

"In December 1935, many strange things happened in the schools. At night boys would go to the classroom and I would hear them crying and praying. People began to dream dreams, based on the Book of Revelation. This sort of thing went on for about a year. Some would set out on a ten-mile walk, weeping and trembling and shuddering, to find Lawrence Barham and Ezekieri; and many found Christ. One had the same experience as Paul. His eyes were physically affected from the glory he had seen and he reached Kabale led by the hand. The atmosphere was charged and those who would not heed were scared and could not sleep. I went to Mr Tribe, the headmaster, with a crowd of other boys, to confess my sin, but I was not converted.

"I left school and was sent to Mbarara high school, where many masters and boys had been converted through Blasio's preaching, but I lost through disobedience a real grounding in the Grace of God. By the time I reached Teacher Training College at Mukono I was in a bad way. In 1940 I came back to Kigezi to teach at the primary school and I found the whole district endowed with tremendous power and joy. Every saved person had been 'mobilized' and men, women and children were evangelizing. All over Kigezi there was the sound of singing and each one sought to bring another. Though most of these people were illiterate, they knew the Lord and each converted person felt responsible for his unsaved relatives. People had taken on a new value, and those who loved Jesus would stop their friends and relatives in the street, and with tears rolling down their faces, plead with them to repent and return to Christ. Hundreds were converted, not by sermons, but by such depths of love. Many were liberated from pagan habits, including witch-doctors and priests, and everywhere you went, tending the cattle or hoeing the fields, you heard people talking about Jesus as a person whom they knew intimately.

"As a schoolteacher I denounced this emotionalism and fanaticism, but they loved me and were concerned for me. I was hard and I hated them, but I knew they were real. My uncle said, 'Religion has become too personal; it invades our privacy; it pushes into every department of our daily life.' There was no special spiritual leader. Everyone depended on the Holy Spirit.

"One evening in October 1941 my sister and my niece, aged fourteen and fifteen, were praying and God told them that I would be restored and saved that week-end. One child came and told me so on Saturday, and on Sunday I heard her tell our household, 'God has answered our prayers for Festo.' I was so angry that I went out and drank all day in my misery, but as I went home that night I met the head of our school coming from the church and he stopped me on the road to put things right with me. I knew then that my friend had found the reality I had missed.

"That night as I struggled alone, Jesus intervened. The Spirit showed me Christ hanging on the Cross. I had a clear sight of Christ dying for me in love. He spoke to me and I heard His voice, 'While you were careless, I still loved you.' That was my forgiveness. I saw a lady and I shouted, 'Jesus has come to me!' That was my liberation and since then I have never stopped witnessing.

"In 1943 I married Merab, and in 1945 the Lord called us to Tanzania, not so much to teach as to share. Many doors opened and things began to move. . . . In 1956 I went to London. I had met many missionaries saved, but not set free, and I did not expect much. I went to share, and I found students hungry and thirsty for God. I am not a good preacher; but I wanted to share the reality of the living Christ, and it opened many people's eyes to see their own lack of reality, an African for whom Jesus had done so much."

Perhaps the war years were some of the most progressive the Mission ever went through, for they tested the reality of all the glowing confessions of the revival. Before such stern, practical demands of self-denial, hard work, added responsibility and dependence on God alone, all that was merely emotional and of man shrivelled up and disappeared, while all that was of God shone out in brighter splendour. Nor was it only in Africa that this spirit of self-sacrifice was manifested. It was seen in Britain where Friends of Ruanda went on giving at a far more costly level; in the splendid work of the home staff who allowed no break in their activities when their office was bombed to the ground, and in the spirit of the children left behind for an indefinite period of time. If Mrs Stanley Smith wavered at the prospect of leaving her four in England with the threat of bombing and invasion hanging over them, Nora soon put her right: "You must go, Mummy," she said, "I will look after the others. Daddy needs you much more than we do."

14

Into All the World

Missionary conventions for the deepening of spiritual life had started in Gisenyi on Lake Kivu in 1938 and 1939, and from 1942 onwards there have been a number of conventions for missionaries of the Protestant Alliance, founded in 1935. These conferences, started during the troubled, divided years of revival, were like spiritual hospitals where wounded spirits were made whole. Barriers were broken down, pride humbled and sin confessed as men and women, often previously estranged, prayed together and pleaded for understanding and reconciliation. Because, even when things were at their worst, they all wanted passionately to see God's way and be reconciled, over and over again light was given and pardon and peace granted.

In 1939 the first African convention was held at Musema, consisting mostly of the *Balokole* or saved ones, as they have now come to be called (their original name was the *Abaka* or the "blazing ones"). These people who had passed through that revival experience of deep conviction of sin and a mighty, over-whelming sense of forgiveness and liberation were clearly recognizable and one of their chief marks was this new desire for fellowship. They loved Christ so much that to find Him looking out of the eyes of another was a sweetness almost too great to be borne, and they manifested their joy in true African fashion. In a land where tribal divisions have made communal trust and fellowship impossible for hundreds of years and where men live out their lives in fear of their neighbours, it was a new and wonderful thing to see men of different tribes and districts thronging together, and greeting each other ecstatically as a great, joyful family, breaking into hymns of praise. It was the very Gospel in action.

Of this easily recognizable, definite class of Christians Dr Stanley Smith wrote, "Those who join them are coming into a community which claims the highest standards of holiness, where the power of the Blood of Jesus is manifestly at work and they know to what they are coming. May the Lord help us never to lower that standard. There are certain things that they have been led to expect of the Protestant Church, and which they will want to see whenever they join us. These things are becoming more and more characteristic of the revived Church and our Africans are finding them very attractive. One is the fellowship meeting, another is team witness, another is a oneness between Europeans and Africans."

This "oneness" was costly to achieve, but it was a big step forward when, in 1943, it was decided that the Protestant Alliance should include members of the African Church, and Kosiya Shalita was elected joint President with Pastor Haley, leader of the Free Methodist Mission. A few months before this election, the first united conference for missionaries and Africans was held at Muyebe.

It was not entirely successful. Every new advance seems to have had its own birth-pangs, and every step forward was bitterly opposed. The convention opened with wild, tumultuous scenes of welcome, as different contingents of Africans arrived from different districts. Emotions ran riot and unrestrained exuberance bordered on hysteria. All that had been so bitterly criticized in the revival was jubilantly enacted before the very eyes of the shocked Europeans and Americans. The African leaders, when begged to restrain the people from these extravagances, utterly refused to do so. "What is the matter with you missionaries?" replied one. "Down there souls are being blessed and saved, but up here you are all anxious and worried." It was hard to accept, but gradually most of the missionaries realized that Africa must express its joy in its own way, and sing to its own rhythm.

Each year brought them nearer to their hard-won goal and 1945 was a memorable year. At the Alliance convention for missionaries at Mutaho, there was a very wonderful spirit of love and unity. None of the Missions made any secret of the difficulties they were going through, and each was surrounded by the prayers of all the rest. They left rejoicing and in September many gathered again for the convention at Kabale.

The team, consisting of about fifty Africans and Europeans, met as usual for a quiet day before the convention and, even at that late hour, there was much to straighten out. The arrangements caused anxiety, too. That great open-air, arena-shaped church, for instance, dug by five hundred voluntary workers to seat five thousand—would it ever be filled? In any case, the weather was appalling, and on Wednesday it was certainly filled—but only with muddy water; and if it ever were filled with people, could any human voice reach out over such a vast space? Those five fifty-foot long buildings for sleeping the delegates—would the delegates come? The Kampala contingent seemed unable to get transport, and the war-time buses were always grossly overloaded.

But the weather cleared and was perfect; the District Commissioner did what seemed quite impossible in war time—granted a permit for two lorries to go and fetch the delegates from Kampala; and two friends provided the funds. A loudspeaker outfit and a microphone were located in Burundi and brought by car over the precipitous, perilous, mountain roads of Rwanda. They arrived just in time, for by the afternoon of the 19th December, people were arriving from all four points of the compass; from Uganda, Rwanda, Burundi, Kenya and Tanzania, and even a small group from the Congo. The sight of those thousands and thousands of people streaming up the hill was a rebuke to the fearful, as though Christ were saying over again, "How is it that ye have no faith?" There were well over seven thousand at the first meeting. Far away on the slopes of the arena, a forest of hands went up as the loud-speaker was turned on and the amazed crowd began to get used to it. A chorus of praise ascended. The conference started with the story of the Lord Jesus feeding the five thousand, and there, in person, He was present again on the hillside, to satisfy these thousands of Africans.

Dr Joe Church described the never-to-be-forgotten Sunday. "The arena had 7,500 seats, but was overflowing long before the service, and still the crowd grew on and on, line after line, right up the hillside to the church and over the sides, till we reckoned there must have been 15,000 people at that service. A few may have come from curiosity, but on the whole they were ordinary, well-dressed church members, coming to a convention for Christians. Singing was difficult at first, but on Sunday, Gregory-Smith played his piano-accordion into the microphone, and the music could be heard to the farthest boundary. Psalm 23 was read followed by a talk by Dr Church, based on verse 5, 'My cup runneth over'.

"Imagery has a great place in African teaching. They pictured each man's heart as a cup: large cups, small cups, old and new, and Christ waiting with the Water of Life to fill each cleansed cup as He passes along. Sometimes He passes by because some of the cups are unclean, or filled to the brim with jealousy, hatred and Self; and Self is a poor drink to take to a thirsty world. But Jesus Himself drank to the dregs the bitter cup of sin. 'The cup that My Father hath given Me, shall I not drink it?'

"The hymn 'Pass me not, Oh gentle Saviour' rose spontaneously from the massed throng, and in William Nagenda's talk that followed he seemed to lead the crowd right back to Calvary, to the place where God turned away His face as Christ drank the cup of bitterness. Many, many were weeping. Then the hymn 'There is life for a look at the crucified One' was started up by a few and gradually taken up, until 15,000 throats swelled the chorus, 'Look, look, look and live.' Faces relaxed and broke into smiles and laughter. Perhaps there was no greater testimony to the reality of the revival than the shining, radiant faces of men and women who told you quite simply that they had seen Jesus."

The testimonies went on and on and on: not only from the big meetings, but from those who gathered in little groups far into the night round the camp-fires, under the shelters and in little homesteads where men sought forgiveness and sang for joy. At the testimony meeting on Sunday afternoon, missionaries and Africans alike told how God had spoken to them. The little pygmy, who had walked for days through the Congo forest, was so short that the microphone had to be lowered for him, but his voice rang out clear and strong: "As I walked to this platform, I was filled with fear, but I have prayed the Lord Jesus to stand by me and He has. All fear has gone and I can tell you what He has done for me."

In the afternoon a crowd gathered singing around the carpenter's shop. At their feet was a fire in which two native harps were burning. Jeremiah, the mission carpenter, had been saved and had called his friends to witness the burning of things used in drinking bouts. Next day he came up to the platform. "I used to work well during the day", he said, "and Europeans praised me, but at sundown I became a different man. I became a demon, shouting, drinking, abusing people, playing heathen songs. It was a life of hypocrisy and I could stand no more, so I have burned my harps and my past. The Devil has gone out; Jesus has come in."

The wife of the senior evangelist said something like this. "You all know we have not been happy in our home. My husband is not right yet, but I have been hard and bad. One day in a meeting, God spoke to me and said, 'Slip your hand into his.' I did, and a new love came into our lives. My husband is not through, but I love him more now and I believe he is coming."

Enthusiastic schoolboys at Shyogwe, Rwanda

Translation in Progress. Joel of the Bembe tribe talks to Rosemary Guillebaud about the first Gospel printed in his language and translated by him

Refugees by the church at Buye, Burundi

African Portrait. ". . . that we may be able to comfort them. . . ."
2 Corinthians 1:4

A rich trader who had spent his life going from one enterprise to another—carpentry, tanning, fishing and smuggling gold—came up the hill with the crowds to see what was going on. Before he went home he was able to say, "Selling hides, selling fish, stealing, lust, even gold, nothing satisfies except Jesus."

It was ten years before another such conference was arranged at Kabale though conventions were held in many other places. Indeed, the special message that God seemed to have imparted so freely and clearly during the revival years was beginning to be carried far afield. It has sometimes been called the "Ruanda message", but there is no monopoly. It is the simple, costly, age-old message that God gave in part to Israel through the mouth of all His prophets and that John the Baptist preached in the wilderness: that humble repentance and reconciliation with God and one's neighbours is the first step toward blessing. It is the message that Jesus emphasized when He said, "Blessed are the poor in spirit . . . Blessed are ye that weep . . . Blessed are ye that hunger and thirst after righteousness," and on these old foundations of true repentance, recognition and confession of sin, they experienced a new conception of fellowship. To let God's light shine on our sin can only cause us to flee to the Cross, and the ground at the foot of the Cross is level. There is only one common denominator there: our need of Jesus because of our sin and pride, and all the barriers, classes and artificialities men have erected melt away. There is only one class at the Cross: humble, forgiven sinners, rejoicing because Jesus has forgiven them and this forms a bond between them that cannot be broken. "If we walk in the light as He is in the light, we have fellowship one with another, and the Blood of Jesus Christ, His Son, cleanseth us from all sin."

This special insight was given at a time when it was most needed. It was the only solution to the age-old social barrier between black and white, missionary and convert. It flared to its logical conclusion during the second World War, the only answer to racial hatred and prejudice. All over the world men who were sick and scarred by fighting, bombing and killing, recognized it; they saw that it worked, and longed to understand the secret. So it came about that in the fifties calls came from far countries and teams of African and English brethren went together to share what God had taught them. In the decade following the end of the war, teams travelled from East Africa to many parts of the world—to India and Pakistan, North America, Brazil, Australia, New Guinea and to various countries in Europe and Africa. Team members included Africans and Europeans: Joe Church, William Nagenda, Yosiya Kinuki, Roy Hession and Festo Kivengere.

It is probably true to say that wherever the teams travelled the message got across, because they went in simple dependence on the Holy Spirit, without trappings or attractions, simply to share what God had taught them. Because they longed for reality and were drawn by sincerity whatever the colour of a man's skin; pride, prejudice, complacency and pretence were broken down, sin was confessed, cold hearts caught fire, estranged parties were reconciled and love and fellowship were restored.

Bonds were forged that nothing could break and without which hatred and party spirit must have prevailed. Dr Church describes how the message was preached in Kenya at the heart of the Mau-Mau rebellion. "It was Sunday morning in Nairobi. We were told that a small convention was taking place on the outskirts of Nairobi in one of the worst Mau-Mau districts. It was organized by the Kikuyu Christians themselves, and we heard they wanted us to join them. Although we understood that it was dangerous for any Europeans to leave the main road, we left it and went a few miles into the heart of the reserve. An amazing sight met us. A vast crowd of about two thousand were sitting, orderly and quiet, on the hillside in a natural open-air arena and the service was being conducted by a team of Kikuyu brethren, everyone of whom is a marked man, and every one of whom faces death daily for his testimony. There was a small platform fitted up with a microphone and loud-speaker. The service had begun when we arrived.

"I was called to sit on the platform beside a Kikuyu clergy-man. His face was scarred and partly paralysed from wounds he had received when he was slashed from head to foot and left for dead for refusing to deny his Lord. Finally, the words 'Mau-Mau' were cut into the flesh of his arm. He smiled as I sat down beside him.

"The crowd grew as people gathered on the outskirts and the time came for the first speaker to preach. He opened his Bible at the Gospel of John and read the text, 'If the Son, there-fore, make you free, ye shall be free indeed.' There was a hush over that great crowd. I looked at the face of the brother who was speaking. It seemed to shine as he talked of his Lord.

" 'I used to be in a prison of fear and hatred of the white man, and now there is the fear of Mau-Mau, but God has shown me the way of freedom because His Son has come to set me free. He has shown me the way to love because He first loved me. I love you, my Kikuyu brothers who are in this bondage of Mau-Mau, and I love the white man, too. It is sin that binds us. Won't you let Him break you and set you free?'

"A chorus of praise rang out again and again, right to the edge of the crowd. It was sung, strange to say, in a language not their own, but in the language of Buganda which they have learnt to love because of the many conventions in the past which they have shared with the brethren in Uganda. It was a little foretaste of heaven when every kindred, tribe and nation will stand before the Throne, and the secret that makes it possible is the same there as here—the Lamb in the midst."

15

The Emergence of Education

It is a far cry from the crowds of skin-clad urchins squatting on the ground while the first patient missionaries traced the alphabet in the dust, to the fine secondary high schools of the sixties, and the slow transition from the one to the other is worth tracing. The early missionaries at Kabale were not entirely without help, as government schools existed in Uganda in the twenties, and as early as 1930, Margaret Forbes wrote excitedly, "Keziya and Agnesi are hoping to sit for the entrance exam to Gayaza Normal School. They are going for two years' training with the promise that they shall teach for two years here afterwards. They will be the first Kigezi girls to be trained."

There were problems, no doubt, but they were probably far less complex than nowadays, and one cannot but think longingly of those comparatively carefree days. The problems consisted mainly of shortage of supplies, lack of equipment and shortage of manpower. The children were crying to be taught, and those pioneers in Christian education, Constance Hornby, Dora Skipper, Margaret Forbes, Jack Warren, Geoffrey Holmes, Jim Brazier and Lawrence Barham found it a heartbreaking job selecting and turning away, and sometimes the persistence of the child itself got the better of them. "Every day the girls besiege us with the query, 'When can we come to school?'" wrote Dora Skipper in 1930. "But alas, each girl costs money to feed and clothe. Two girls ran away from their homes and came to us, hearing there was a place of refuge where they could learn, because at home they were persecuted and beaten for trying to learn at the nearest church. Although the school is not built and we had nowhere to keep them, we had not the heart to refuse this piteous appeal."

The aims of the old missionaries were simple, too: education not for its own sake, but as a means of evangelization and teaching the Christian faith. "Our aim is not an educated African aristocracy, but a consecrated ministry of teachers, clergy and civil servants," wrote Jim Brazier in 1930. "We do not want a religious distinction to exist between government workers and mission workers. We want to exercise our ministry of evangelism through both." And how well they succeeded in those early years, as one after another went out, content with the merest pittance of pay, to open little out-schools all over the district. "We want to go and work in the new stations," said four eager little twelve-year-olds to Muriel Barham, and it was only with the greatest difficulty that she made them see that they were rather too young, as yet.

Because of this, offers of help from the Government were viewed with caution. "We had a visit from the Chief Inspector of schools today," wrote Jim Brazier, "and the whole question of our Teachers' School will have to be reconsidered. It was started as a training school for evangelists and that is its real function. The Government gave us a grant to encourage it and now a special syllabus. They are keen to help as best they can, but their aim and object doesn't always coincide with ours."

Yet they made conscientious efforts to train their teachers. In 1932 the first three girls from Rwanda to receive a teacher's training travelled up to Toro, and Lawrence Barham insisted on his boys taking the government teachers' certificate. Then Joy Gerson, in 1936, selected seven promising girls from Kigeme and took them to Gahini, where she and Miss Skipper could train them in their own methods and inculcate their own aims.

"Miss Skipper helped me to start the Kigeme school while I was still at Gahini," wrote Joy Gerson. "She had built us a hut in the school compound and now we have seven girls getting ready. Would you pray for these seven girls? If they are filled with the Holy Spirit, they will be real missionaries; if they only have a head knowledge and say things because they don't want to be different from the others at Gahini, they will be no help at all."

The Kigeme school followed a pattern all of its own and was wonderfully successful spiritually and, according to the standards of its day, educationally. Joy Gerson, with the help of Mrs Hindley and the seven Gahini teachers, started by teaching about eighty children out of doors, owing to lack of any building. The six months of the rainy season made this difficult, so they pressed on in huts, specially concentrating on the older girls who would soon be married and go to the surrounding districts. "Pray for these first," wrote Joy, "that they may become really equipped soldiers of the Lord Jesus before they become teachers' wives and go to lonely places full of temptation. Please pray for them, that they won't run away from the claims of Jesus. There is no knowing what might happen through a few girls really on fire. We are realizing that unless God's children are on fire and have no barriers between themselves and Him, and between themselves and each other, those outside will never be won."

Her "School Council" was a new departure, too, consisting of four parents and four teachers who discussed every problem together; the finance, the choice of teachers or hospital trainees. It went a long way toward building up mutual confidence and making the Africans feel that the school was their own project. Perhaps it was because of this that she soon gained the trust of the ruling Tutsi class, and the local chief sent his seven little daughters to be educated.

Girls were growing up saved, knowing God, and ready to take their place as missionary teachers. There was a special afternoon, during the war years when missionary personnel was at its lowest, and schools were crying out for help. Joy and her older girls met on a hillside and asked God to show them which girls were to stay and teach at Kigeme, which were to go and run the out-schools and which three were to leave home and travel south across the border into a new country, and help to open the new school at Buye. Happily, they were all given one mind about it, an echo of the old apostolic days when they met to pray and fast, and the Holy Spirit said, "Separate Me Barnabas and Saul"—only these delegates were not strong apostles, just teenagers from rural Rwanda.

It was a system suited to the times, but the times were changing, and the war brought such a violent transition to the country that only the Hand of God over the Mission could have moved swiftly and surely enough to keep pace. One big problem at that period was the education of the missionary children. It was impossible to send them home at that point, so in 1940 a small establishment was founded. Eileen Faber, who had been teaching four little boys in a garage, Marion Bowie and Joan Brewer, who had been teaching the Jackson and the Buxton children, combined to start the Kabale Preparatory School. It developed rapidly. At first it was a private venture, but in 1947 the Mission took over responsibility for it. In 1952, the Uganda Government recognized the school and provided for its rebuilding, and now it stands, a gracious house with a welcoming porch from which two carved rabbits look out from above the lintel. It is surrounded by wide green lawns and great trees that are perfect for climbing, and beyond the lawns the hills slope down into deep valleys, filled with mists in the morning, which gradually disperse like filmy curtains as the sun rises in the sky. In this haven of beauty among the hills, hundreds of little boys and girls have grown from the ages of six to ten in a happy home atmosphere. Missionaries send their children from all over Rwanda, Burundi and Uganda, and more and more Indian traders and African government officials, Protestants and Catholics and even a few Muslims, are entering theirs. There are no racial barriers, and the children forget the colour of each other's skin and probably learn for life that valuable lesson of Christian brotherhood. On the first day of term, they run in and greet Nan Read and the other teachers as old, loved friends, and then away, with never a backward look, to the swings and the trees. "This is a Jesus school," wrote one little boy during his first term. "It's fun!"

But it was not only missionary children who needed educating during those war years. A hurricane of Western ideas began to blow into primitive Africa and with it came a sudden burning desire for education. "The whole country has gone mad in a rush for learning," wrote one. "Africa has been drawn into the comity of nations, and to take her place she must be educated. Schools are the only way to progress, so in Rwanda and Burundi education, hitherto left entirely in the hands of the missionaries—Catholic or Protestant, has now become an important part of government planning." Gone in a few years were the days when families were grateful for their children to learn from untrained missionaries and to make do with their inadequate equipment—the missionaries' ultimate aim being to further the Gospel. A new note was now beginning to be heard on all sides, the cry for education on an advanced level from qualified teachers; and the loudest cry came from the Christians, the saved, revived *Balokole*, who saw daily the sacrifices the missionaries were making to enable their own children to have the best education available, and who had been awakened by Christianity to the importance of every aspect of their children's lives, body, soul and spirit.

A new era had dawned and, once again, God had foreseen and prepared. The Church's services to the country in time of famine and epidemic had commended it, not only to the respectable, ruling Tutsi, but also to the colonial Government, who now regarded it as a force to be reckoned with. And now, more than ever, as nationalism began to raise its head, men felt

the blessings of the fellowship between black and white. The
new day, with its challenges and potential dangers, was faced
together by those who had become a band of brothers and
sisters; colour, class and tribe swallowed up in the unity of the
people of God. And to this solid, rock-like community, widespread over the country, the Government turned in its per-
plexity, demanding schools for higher education. People of all
classes turned to it, believing that it possessed the secret of
happy, victorious living. A number of the old-style educationalists had gone home, leaving a rich, spiritual harvest and
empty places in the schools. Few were coming out, but Peter
Guillebaud came in that most improbable year 1939, and he
and his wife, Elisabeth, fully qualified educationalists, possessed
the vision and ability that were needed. Their first act was to
hold two successive two-year training courses for schoolmasters at Buye, without which those opening doors could
never have been entered. These men gained a knowledge of
teaching methods and the ground to be covered in a Belgian
Ecole Primaire, and were to be the backbone of the schools for
years to come.

When, in 1946, the Belgian Government of Rwanda and
Burundi revised its educational policy, it offered Protestant
missions equal grants and opportunities with those given
hitherto only to Roman Catholics, if they were willing to sign
the educational agreement. Under this convention, schools had
to be subject to government inspection, follow the government
syllabus, and bring teaching staff into conformity with Belgian
standards. European teachers had to have a good knowledge of
French, spend a year in Belgium and pass an examination. No
restrictions were placed upon religious teaching, and the Mission, in common with the whole Protestant Alliance, signed
the convention. To refuse would have meant handing over the
whole youth of the country to the Roman Catholics.

The "good old days" were over and the missionaries found
themselves swept into a vortex of inspections, reports, regis-

ters, statistics and examination programmes. Some may have felt regretful, but to the new young teachers it was a tremendous challenge and opportunity. The Guillebauds, in simple thatched buildings with the minimum of equipment, started their school on the new site at Shyogwe in 1946. It was planned as a central boarding school for promising boys, to train them up to standard for admission to the government secondary school at Butare. Two years later they also opened the first *Ecole des Moniteurs* (Teacher Training College) to provide the four-year training needed for the Primary Teacher diploma.

All through the forties the schools were overflowing with eager, ambitious lads and, more and more, the Government was looking to the Missions to play their part in the huge advance programme. Dr Stanley Smith was appointed a member of the *Conseil du Gouvernement*; also of the Provincial Council of the Welfare Fund.

At Shyira, Joy Gerson and Mabel Jones laid the foundations of co-education by running a teachers' training course for boys and girls. At Matana, Lindesay Guillebaud opened people's eyes to the importance of kindergarten work. It had not occurred to the average African that their four- and five-year-olds were worth such attention. "I have 90 three- to ten-year-olds," she wrote, "who come every morning, bringing their fees in the form of cow dung for manure, or firewood. Their parents won't pay any money for them, so they practise self-help."

Up in the Kigezi district of Uganda, where the English language was the stepping-stone to advancement, things moved even faster. The Kigezi High School was now part of a fully-organized educational system with one of its own old boys as headmaster, and successful scholars could pass on to a college in Kampala or, within a few years, to English universities. The decade of the fifties found many of the post-war problems assuming increasing proportions. As the novelty of higher education wore off, so the steady rat-race continued. There was the problem of overcrowding, poor, inadequate buildings, lack of modern equipment and insufficiently trained teachers. There was the bottle-neck of secondary education, when the vast majority of children who had been through primary school and had woken up to the advantages of learning, had to return to the hills and cultivate the land.

As late as 1953 many teachers had no textbooks and, apart from the New Testament, Protestant literature was almost non-existent. Many young people, thirsty to read, were turning to the Roman Catholics for supplies. There was also the problem of finding truly dedicated, single-minded Christian teachers, who would stand apart from factions and politics. "Since all the schools are mission schools, either Protestant or Catholic," wrote T. G. Gregory-Smith, "the educated, influential people are all nominal Christians and strong denominational loyalties and politics are carried into social life. Beneath an often calm surface are strong cross-currents and intrigues. Only the truly saved do not get engulfed in strife and enmity."

As a result of all this, there was the new, increasing spirit of resentment, ambition and materialism to contend with in staff and children alike. "As opportunities for learning increase, the interest in the Gospel becomes less and less, and even smaller children are impatient of anything that seems to them of no material value," wrote an African headmaster, and the cry of nearly all was epitomized by the comment of a boy in the high school of Butare: "The people who matter in this country are those who are sufficiently well-educated to take a leading part in the social and political life of the country. Why don't you Protestants make a greater effort to get more of us well-educated so that we can make our presence felt?"

It was certainly not for lack of effort. Missionaries were battling, often single-handed, to begin to solve these problems. Even the medicals were turning from their overcrowded hospitals to build and man the new schools. Dr Goodchild toiled daily from one hill-top to another between his ward rounds to build the girls' school at Kigeme and Dr Stanley Smith, well-known as being able to turn his hand to anything, took over the headmastership of Shyogwe during the Guillebauds' furlough and afterwards became first warden of the Protestant boys' home at Butare, where there was a large Roman Catholic secondary school, available to boys who passed the entrance exam from Shyogwe. "My teaching is limited to French, hygiene, singing, and higher maths," he wrote complacently!

On the literature side Peter and Elisabeth Guillebaud spent hours drawing up a syllabus, with adequate notes, when text-books were still lacking. Physical and mental effort was being expended, perhaps as never before, so much so that some questioned the right of it, and young missionaries coming out from England were sometimes thoroughly perplexed. "I have learned a good many things in the past year", wrote Joan Nicholson, "from pruning of coffee trees to smocking, from mass dyeing of school frocks to accounts, from bulk food buying to gym and dancing to gramophone records."

Dick Lyth, when headmaster of the Kigezi High School, was coping with language study, the spiritual care of the European community, and numerous pastoral duties connected with a living, overflowing church. His diary gives a glimpse of some of the daily problems. "A new week, full of the multifarious requests and questions which are part of the pattern of life for a headmaster in Africa. Such things as: 'Please, sir, I'm sick.'

" 'What's the matter?'

" 'I've got pneumonia in my ear, sir.'

" 'Well, go over to my wife. She'll fix it for you.'

" 'Please, sir, who was Cain's wife, sir?'

" 'I don't know. Tuck your shirt in, boy.'

" 'Please, sir, are politics a good thing, or a bad thing?'

" 'Both. Where's your belt, boy?'

" 'It got taken by a bird, sir. It thought it was a snake, sir.'

" 'No! I won't believe that story; not even once! . . . Come to my office after school.'

The Emergence of Education

"My prayer (aside): 'Oh, Lord, I love these boys. Give me more patience. Please keep my vision clear. Help me, in the midst of frustrations and multitudinous duties and problems, always to see them as boys for whom You died, and as potential leaders in this country and in the Kingdom of God. Help me to be an example. For Christ's sake, Amen.' "

That, to the missionaries, was the great, pulsing heart of the problem. "Help me to see them as boys for whom You died. Help me to be an example." And the answer to that lay in their personal contact with the Lord Jesus, and in the resulting strength and integrity of their daily lives. A great deal of time could no longer be given to that which was purely "spiritual", and some succumbed, and are still succumbing, to the deep discouragement of thinking that the grind of pushing girls and boys through examinations was *not* what they came to do, and was not really worth while. And yet, where men and women walked with God, the "secular" was transformed and boys and girls glimpsed Christ. What mattered in these circumstances was not the time spent on conventions and evangelization, but that supreme, final purpose of God for every Christian, "That they might be conformed to the image of His Son."

"With such a family to control and lead almost single-handed," wrote Kenneth Kitley (eighty-six boys in very crowded conditions, forty-two seniors studying in their dormitories with piles of books between the beds), "I'm continually cast on Jesus alone for taking prayers. He must come between me and each boy with his differing thoughts and moods. God has provided Jesus for all our need, and He means Him to be essential all day long. Pray that we may never be swamped by routine work, and our busyness may not make us dry and cold. May we take Jesus and His burning love to these lovable children."

And where that love burned and men and woman lived close enough to Jesus to know His will and delight in the doing of it, there was a steady rise in academic results and true spiritual results in the community. Joan Nicholson at Shyogwe, commented on the opportunities that arose in class. "I have been amazed in our discussions at the many opportunities there have been to point to Christ as the only solution to our problems. In psychology lessons they have asked, 'Can character really be changed or does it depend mostly on heredity?' 'If a person is very sensitive and easily hurt by nature, what can he do about it?' 'If someone is born with a bad temper, is it his fault?'

"On another occasion we were discussing the moral development of the child, and in conclusion I said that one of the greatest things they could do for the children they would be teaching, would be to pray for them. This caused quite a stir, as if they had never heard of such an idea. Amid other comments, one girl said under her breath, 'But why? You don't pray for us, do you?'

" 'How do you know that I don't?'

" 'Do you?'

" 'Yes.'

" 'We're very glad to know that,' said one.

" 'What do you pray for us?' asked an attractive lad.

" 'That depends on the individual, but the first thing I pray is that you will all be saved.' He digested this for a second and then said, quite politely:

" 'Suppose God doesn't answer your prayers, what then?'

"I tried not to get too deeply involved in predestination in my reply," comments Joan Nicholson, "but please join your prayers with mine that many of these boys and girls may be saved."

The Guillebauds tell of a Saturday morning at Buye when there was no school. The rain had put a stop to hoeing. Peter had planned to spend most of the day under his car, repairing a spring. The boys were sitting in their dormitory. For days they had felt unhappy, convicted; and now they covenanted to remain there, praying and fasting, until the Lord met with them. What really happened in that "upper room" was never fully revealed, but sinners were saved, Christians were reconciled and sins were confessed. They appeared late in the evening, their faces bright with the glory of their new experience. Next day, they lit a bonfire where letters of an immoral character and a blanket stolen from a lorry were publicly burnt, and the hymn they had composed together the day before, rang out in power. It was based on *Pilgrim's Progress* and the chorus:

> *Blest Cross, Blest Sepulchre, Blest rather be,*
> *The Man that there was put to death for me,*

was soon reverberating through the country.

Yes, amid the rubbish and noise of worldly ambition and materialism, God's building was going up, small, but strong and sound. The foundations of Christian character were being laid in the classrooms, in the playing fields, in the daily contacts with the boys and girls, and many became true Christians. The world looked on critically and failed to understand, but perhaps one of the most striking testimonies to the work of those years was given by a Governor-General of the Congo in the year 1954. "The educational work of Protestant Missions remains an enigma. On the one hand we see poor, inadequate buildings and insufficient knowledge of French and rudimentary teaching methods; on the other hand, many completely unbiased sources such as mines, commerce, the army, and intellectuals, all bear testimony to the high moral character of the pupils leaving these schools. What is the answer to this enigma? It must be the close association of the master and the pupils, the voice of the heart speaking to the heart."

But the tired teachers, struggling to keep themselves from being completely immersed in the problems and to hold fast to their priorities, knew another answer.

16

The Development of the Medical Work

Once again it is a far, far cry from the first dispensaries and hospitals held in tents and grass huts, to the relatively orderly, efficient hospitals of the sixties. Young medicals and nurses straight from England still get a shock; but for their cheer, let us look back to the beginning and see what they missed.

Meet Mr Jackson with his early problems at Gahini: "Every day from forty to fifty patients come in from miles around for such poor treatment as we can give them. Our medical buildings are two small huts; one will hold five people, so close that they touch one another, and the other, about the same size, has a single shelf of drugs and forms our dispensary and operating theatre. Can you imagine a dozen people sitting round a single bowl of disinfectant and dipping little pieces of wool into it to wash ulcers, sometimes the size of your hand? You who know anything of hygiene will be horrified at the thought, but this is the best we can do for them at present, and it is surprising how well some of them respond to the treatment." His quiet remark that it was a relief to welcome Dr Joe Church, a fully qualified doctor, sounds like the understatement of the year.

The lack of amenities and equipment of those early days taxed their ingenuity to the utmost. We have a sketch of Dr Stanley Smith amputating a gangrenous leg in a mud-hut home with the help of "a saw, a hammer, a chisel boiled in a bucket, a few artery forceps, some needles and thread and a clergyman

Billy Graham greeted by Dr J. E. Church and the Rev Festo
Kivengere on arrival in Burundi for a campaign in 1960

Loving Care. Dr Jeffrey Newth examining a baby

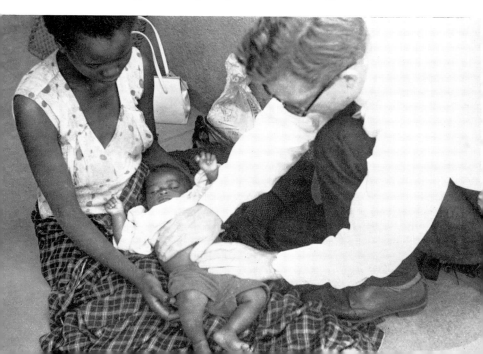

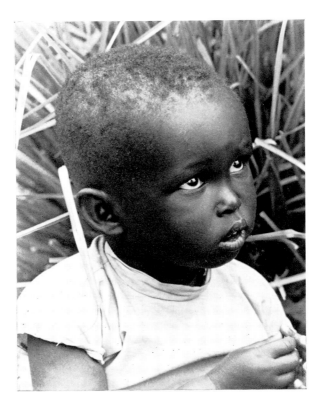

What does the future hold?

Radio Cordac, Bujumbura. A Gospel disc jockey

giving the anaesthetic." A woman, who grunted alarmingly at each respiration following an attack of pleurisy, was taken to the garage. Dr Stanley Smith started up a car engine, and by connecting the terminals of one of the sparking plugs she received a powerful series of shocks through her throat and chest and was cured in a moment. Varicose ulcers were bandaged with the strips of rubber from old inner tubes of car tyres.

The impossibility of coping with all that turned up, the wearing choice of trying to achieve the impossible or leaving someone to die, often resulted in appalling overcrowding. "Outpatients have risen to two hundred a day," wrote Bill Church from Buhiga, "and we operate six times a week. All this is carried on in a small dispensary and the first block of our future hospital, consisting of two small wards, one for women, one for men. The floors are laid with hay and the patients lie as thick as sardines. They don't mind the crush at all. In fact, it keeps them warm, and the majority go home cured."

It was not only the doctors who suffered. It was just as hard for the nurses. Mildred Forder gives a picture of the somewhat frustrating conditions that prevailed in Gahini in 1935: "The hospital was pretty primitive when I first went to Gahini. For instance, one day some weeks after my arrival, I discovered that the fomentations which had been ordered four-hourly were not being done. In my limited language, I inquired why this was so, and was told there was no hot water. (Had it been the dry season, there might well have been no water at all for in those days every drop had to be carried up from the lake at the bottom of the hill.) So I sent for the old lady, an ex-ulcer patient who lived near, to ask her why she had not been heating the water for treatments. She just replied, 'No wood. Didn't you know?' Next, I sent for the one-legged man who looked after the wood. Why hadn't he supplied Sara with the wood she needed to heat the water? 'Oh,' he said, 'there's no wood; the store is empty. Didn't you know?' I tried again. 'Why is the store empty? Aren't the men bringing in the right number of bundles of wood from the bush every day?' 'Oh, no. There is a pride of lions in the place where they get the wood, so the men are afraid to go there. Didn't you know?' So, apparently, it was the lions' fault that the treatments weren't done and I ought to have known that."

Medically, it must have been both repulsive and fascinating. The patients came in hundreds, clothed in filthy skins; the tubercular, the ulcerated and those suffering from leprosy and yaws, malaria and tick fever. There were the casualties from wild beasts, too: "A man attacked by a man-eating lion, a little child whose arm had been almost severed when a hyena tried to pull her from her mother's arms; a girl bathing in the river when a crocodile caught her by the arm. All her friends ran away, but she fought it alone in the water until it had bitten her arm right off, just below the shoulder. She was carried in through wild bush country for several days, arriving in a very bad state, with three inches of splintered bone protruding from the stump. I operated on the stump, but for several days we felt there was no hope for her life. Much prayer was made for her, and she made a complete recovery despite erysipelas and has gone home.

"A heap lying on the grass! On looking closer we realized it was a boy put outside a hut to die. He was nothing but skin and bone. For months he's huddled in his hut, suffering from fever. So long, indeed, that his knees had become permanently bent and he could only crawl. He was carried into hospital and after some time his fever was cured. By a series of operations, we straightened his legs and now you would not recognize him. He looks fat and happy as he hobbles round the compound, learning to walk again. When I realize that the happiness is not simply due to returning health, but to the knowledge of Christ he's learned in the wards, then I feel that all is worth while.

"We have a little girl now, whose mother said she had an

evil spirit inside her which was killing her. I brought her in and certainly for days she was like a mad thing, and screamed with pain, and then would lie exhausted. We watched her closely and then discovered it was tobacco. No doubt from her baby days she had been drugged with it and it was giving her an illness. We fed her up on a sort of barley water and honey, and in six weeks she was like an ordinary girl."'

Little by little, proper rooms with tile or corrugated iron roofs began to replace the thatched mud huts, and beds replaced the hay on the floor, and the doctors arrived to man the hospitals. In the famine year, Gahini hospital had become famous all over Rwanda, and in 1934, the Belgian Government granted the English doctors the status of *Médicin Agrée* and offered them grants and generous aid. Popularity soared, and in 1937 the new hospital at Matana, designed and built by Dr Sharp, was opened in the presence of the King of Burundi and many Belgian officials.

At Gahini, Kigeme and Shyira in Rwanda, and at Buye, Buhigi and Matana in Burundi, the desperately overworked nurses and doctors continued to treat thousands of needy cases and to do relief work on an enormous scale during the 1943–4 famine years. Their influence and scope increased all the time. Government-sponsored maternity and baby clinics brought women from a wide radius.

In Uganda things were rather different, and quite early on there were efficient government clinics and hospitals. In the late thirties it was clear that Kabale hospital was no longer a necessity, yet the closing of it in 1939 caused dismay in the district. The people felt they had lost a spiritual home, and this feeling persisted in spite of increased government facilities, until at last it seemed as though their plea was a call of God and a site was found in 1955 about thirty miles from Kabale, which was ideal in every way for a new hospital. It lay at the head of a valley, surrounded by steep hills thickly populated, a patchwork of cultivated slopes and lush grass where cattle grazed. The building in question had been used as a flax factory, and there was already an electric turbine installed, powered by a ninety-foot waterfall in the woods behind, so the air is moist and smells of water and green growth.

The local people were only too eager for a hospital, but the Government was undecided. For three years the Church waited and prayed while the Government deliberated, but in March 1958 a telegram was handed in at Kabale saying, "Kisiizi is yours."

Great was the joy of the African Church. Thousands flocked there on 30th March to hold a dedication service on the site, and their overwhelming praise was not only for the new hospital. It was as much for their new doctor, John Sharp, son of their deeply loved founder, born in their midst and brought up with their own children, speaking their own language, who stood beside his father. He had come back to serve them in this new capacity and to live among them.

He was, indeed, in a special way a child of promise and their own. His parents had waited so long for the little son to take the place of Robin, and from the first he seems to have been a particularly attractive baby, with his father's own determined lower jaw and wide, engaging smile; and perhaps because God knew that his days were numbered, he was called early, like Samuel, and began to serve God while he was still a little child. He was only seven years old when he truly accepted Christ, and insisted on standing up at a service numbering two or three hundred children and telling them, in perfect Kirundi, that the Lord Jesus was his Saviour and that he wanted them all to love Him, too. He seemed to pass through school without the usual spiritual setbacks, and when he was eighteen years old, he went to the Keswick Convention and knew God wanted him as a missionary and dedicated his life to that calling.

It could have been written of him, "This one thing I do." He trained as a doctor at St Thomas' Hospital and qualified M.B., B.S., in 1954. During those years in London he became the leader of the Inter-Hospital Christian Union, and many testify to the influence of this purposeful, consecrated young man. He became engaged to Doreen Harris, a physiotherapy student, and together they prayed and planned, uncertain of God's leading. When the need of the Kisiizi hospital was put before them, they refused at first. Perhaps it seemed too easy, too obvious, but gradually they felt sure that this was the call of God, and in 1957 John returned with Doreen and their baby, Andrew, and were ready on the spot when the site was given.

John inherited his parents' amazing practical ability, but the building was a family affair. While John and Doreen lived in the old factory, Dr and Mrs Len Sharp camped in their little caravan and, together, father and son measured out the site, planned and supervised the building and revived the generator, while Esther Sharp laid out the beautiful grounds and planted the jacaranda trees. Large, motherly, undaunted by any circumstances, unable ever to learn the language properly, but managing very well with a strange composite language of her own (which she herself called "Esther-anto" and her houseboys patiently learned), wherever Mrs Sharp went, wildernesses blossomed into gardens and deserts became civilized, social and homelike.

So the hospital was opened and there followed eight hard, golden years. John was a capable surgeon and with the co-operation of the staff, the reputation of the hospital soared. Margaret and Christopher were born and the growing family drew the other little children in the district, and John and Doreen's hearts were open to them all. They had a great, shared burden for the children and young people and began to train their Christian workers in Sunday school and Boys' Brigade work. Spiritually, too, the work flourished. Hospital orderlies and patients turned to Christ. "He was a father in God to us," said one old dresser, and the people all over the district echoed the thought. He was their own, a child of the land.

His final illness started while still in Africa, with spells of dizziness and headache and momentary loss of memory. After a preliminary examination at Mulago he was flown to his own hospital, St Thomas', where a tumour of the brain was diagnosed. He was operated on without avail, and medical treatment offered no hope of recovery. Although divine healing was sought, it was not given in this world, but perhaps the answer to that prayer lay in other ways in which God gave grace: to John, facing the great suffering of the last weeks with such victorious courage and peace; to his father, who having recently lost his wife, flew home to be with his son at the end, and who was able to say, "He gave me all. If He asks of me my greatest treasure, shall I withhold it?" And to Doreen, who went back alone with the three children to carry on for two years another task that had been near to her husband's heart, the encouraging of Sunday schools and Scripture Union work in the schools.

In 1963 Robin Church, another child of the land, came out with his wife Joan, and their little daughter, to reopen Kabarole Hospital at Fort Portal in Uganda. Rebuilt by his father, Dr Joe Church, it was an old C.M.S. hospital started by Sir Albert Cook. Twenty thousand pounds were donated by the Government and the opening ceremony took place in 1965, when Princess Margaret herself took the front door key and declared the hospital open. Bishop Erica Sabiti held a short dedication service, and prayer was offered in each department as the royal party toured the buildings. Natural, and thoroughly interested, the Princess lingered in the children's ward to talk to the little patients. Then she and her husband signed the visitors' book "Margaret and Snowdon", the plaque was unveiled and they were gone, leaving an unforgettable memory.

Adequate training schools for the nurses have developed slowly. The first Kabale orderlies came down from Kampala with some training; a number of them drawn to this savage, rolling country by their personal love for Dr Sharp, whom they had known in the Great War. "My enlistment in the Uganda Medical Corps was like the making of bricks," wrote Erisa, one of the oldest, finest nurses. "For the work of nursing was one which I despised above all others, but when I was taken ill with meningitis, Dr Sharp's visits to me were the voice of Jesus calling me to be His workman, even as I am still. And thus it was that when Dr Sharp gave up his time for strolling in the streets at 5 p.m. to visit me, I was filled with joy and forgot my pain. His conversation was as the voice of Jesus." Similarly, a team from Kabale volunteered for Gahini, and a team from Gahini manned Shyira and Kigeme. But as each hospital opened, it became a simple training school for young men and girls learning to be nurses, orderlies, laboratory assistants and dispensers, many of them becoming, over the years, highly skilled. In 1941 Mildred Forder began to train girls as midwives, with such valuable results that in 1949 the enterprise was transferred to Buye to become the Alliance Maternity Training School. Belgian funds financed the buildings and equipment and the girls had to sit for a State examination for a government diploma at the end of a two-year course.

So each year a steady little stream of trained nursing aides and midwives was fed back into the Mission hospitals and a number of these returned with a real care for the spiritual and evangelistic side, and God's work goes steadily on in the hospitals through the witness of selfless, dedicated lives, and through the Word of God. Many, many scenes come into view over the panorama of the years.

1928. The old herdsman of the King of Ankole, breaking through the crowd of rather phlegmatic listeners, and falling at Dr Stanley Smith's feet and clasping his ankles. "When I was taken ill", he cried, "I tried in vain for relief from our heathen medicine men, and when they failed me, I came along to the hospital of the Almighty, for this is His hospital, isn't it? And He has made me well, for wasn't it He who gave you the wisdom?"

1937. A boy bitten by a snake, and Cecil Verity lancing the

swollen hand at a village church, fifty miles from Gahini. The father promised to bring him next day, but as he did not come, Mr Verity set off to find him. He traced the kraal and found the boy, minus bandages, smeared all over with cow dung and covered with flies. Mr Verity's wrath exploded and he told the father what he thought of him in no uncertain terms. Several years later the father walked into his office. "Do you remember being so angry with me?" he said. "From that day I gave up all heathen practices and started going to the church school. Now I want to be baptized." He had learnt to read, and his wife and boy, hand completely restored in spite of the cow dung, were asking for baptism, too.

1937. A middle-aged man sitting in the lantern light at the hospital office, his face set as Dr Bryan and Yosiya tell him that his cancer is inoperable and he is going home to die; and tell him, too, of the Saviour who died, of the life beyond death and the home where there is no pain. Simply, as a child, he kneels with Yosiya in prayer and gives himself up to God through Christ.

1950. A girl of fifteen, disliked and half starved by her step-mother, carried to hospital because the family could no longer stand the smell of her enormous, untreated, tropical ulcer. Slowly she improved, and every day she heard of Jesus and was transformed by believing that there was Someone who loved her and would care for her as long as life lasted. She became cook at the girls' school, a bright, happy girl who loves to tell about her Saviour.

1954. Old Abraham, who can neither read nor write, but whose face just radiates the love of God, is hobbling round the ward showing the other patients his wordless book. "He sits up in his bed", said the night nurse, "and talks to the Lord just as though he was chatting to the man in the next bed; pleading with Him to save those around him, then he turns to the other patients and says, 'I have just been talking to my friend Jesus.'"

1968. A child of ten, the light of her father's eyes, died suddenly under anaesthetic, but for days before her operation her father, a pagan, had sat beside her bed quietly watching what went on in that hospital ward. He marvelled at the patience of a young, visiting medical student, who spent much time and gentle care on a dying old grannie, and when his child was carried back from the theatre and there was nothing to be done but to take her home and bury her, an African nurse gave him a cloth to wrap her in and asked for no pay. The doctor himself gave him a cup of tea and the sister, Elspeth Cole, spared him the long tramp over the hills with the little body in his arms and drove him home in the car. Numbed and bewildered, he made no sign of gratitude and it was not till after the funeral that he talked to his Christian wife. "Look at the love," he kept on saying, "look at the love! What would happen to me if I died suddenly like that?"

"It is like when I plant a bean in my field," said his wife, telling the story later. "It dies there in the ground, but there is a harvest. My child will live again, and my husband is turning to Christ."

So the twin battle of physical and spiritual healing goes on, and doctors and nurses need to be spiritual warriors, strong in body, sound in mind, able and willing to turn their hands to anything.

Many nurses, in the absence of a doctor, have had to perform major operations in order to save life. In 1964 when Dr Henderson left for furlough, Kigeme Hospital, which serves over two hundred thousand people, was left without a resident doctor. Miss Rosemary Preston, S.R.N., agreed to stay on alone and such is the confidence that the people have in the nursing Sisters, that the hospital wards remained full and the clinics drew large numbers.

The arguments in favour of carrying on mission hospitals as better-equipped government centres increased, were often discussed, but in 1955 there was no doubt about the answer. At a medical conference at Kigeme, those present were challenged by the question, "What is your calling?" The following are extracts from some of the replies. "We are certainly treating more patients than ever before. Our calling is not to compete with the expanding government medical work with its first-class equipment and increasing efficiency. What then is our calling? It's the Lord's own way of treating the sick. We are to be spiritual specialists, treating the spiritual as well as the physical, as the spiritual is often the root cause of bodily suffering. As a united team, black and white, we work together for the healing of spirit, mind and body. A new class of disease is springing up all over the world, sometimes called stress diseases, which come from the rush of modern life. They are already with us in Africa, and they call for treatment of the whole man. We believe that, more than at any time in the world, there is the need for Christian hospitals that can deal with the spiritual as well as the physical, and this is the permanent place of the mission hospital."

17

The Growth of the Church

"I went on safari with my wife and baby Mary. We covered nearly two hundred miles and at nearly every place where we camped, we found a witness for Christ. . . . Two lions popped their heads in from the grass not far from where we rested. . . . Our sleep was constantly disturbed by the roaring of lions, the moan of hyenas, the horrible noise of hippos fighting. One of the servants accidentally set fire to our camp. We saved baby Mary and the tents, but we lost many valuable things" (Dr Sharp, 1925).

"A trip round the 'parish' took three weeks, marching on average fifteen miles a day. In some of the sheltered, marshy places, mosquitoes were so thick that they could work in relays. The fun really began, however, about sundown when life outside a net, for a white man at any rate, became impossible. The last meal was taken in bed, pushing the food between the net and the gaps. Within a fortnight of sending out four new young teachers, we hear that all four are down with malaria, but we hope they will become immune" (Dr Stanley Smith, 1927).

"In searching for church sites, there has been a lot of wading through swamps of deep, black, hot, slimy mud. A false step, and in one goes up to one's thighs, waist, or further if unlucky. Then comes the indignity of being hauled out by the guides, but dignity goes to the wind when the alternative is to be left there, stuck fast. Sometimes in the midst of a dense, papyrus swamp we meet a deep, swift, tea-coloured river of three or four yards wide. We strip, tie our clothes into bundles, throw them across the river, swim it, dress on the other side and carry on, slowly wading and pushing our way through at the rate of about half a mile an hour. What a game! And the mud looks, and feels, so foul and shows up so on a white man's skin. Yet all the discomfort is forgotten when we reach a village teeming with needy people—until we remember that we have got to get home again" (Mr Jackson, 1938).

"One day I walked a long distance to a small church. It was the teacher's hut, and I was told there were no readers. I saw some people working close by and asked them why they did not read, and they said, 'We are heathen.' I persuaded them to come to the hut: a man, two women and two boys, and for the first time in my life I experienced the thrill of telling of Jesus to those who never before had heard His name. I told them, as well as I could, who Jesus is and of His undying love to them. I sang . . . 'Yes, Jesus loves me,' and I made them sing it, too. We visited one or two other kraals and urged the people to come and hear the Good News" (Lawrence Barham, 1930).

Against this romantic aura of wild beasts, fire, swamps, flood and mosquitoes, the early missionaries carried on their work of shepherding and building up the village churches that had sprung up all over the district around the mission centres, and the care and instruction of their teachers, some of whom were themselves semi-illiterate and very ignorant. It was not ideal.

In the early days, leadership and control were largely in the hands of missionaries, black and white. At first, all the evangelists and senior teachers were African missionaries from Uganda to Rwanda and from Uganda and Rwanda to Burundi. Among the first Christians in each new district, some would volunteer as evangelists, and with little or no training, they would be sent to start new churches near their homes. Each evangelist was given a junior assistant preparing for baptism, who when baptized, would himself branch off to found another church. But as early as possible at each mission centre, evangelists' training schools were founded where young volunteers could receive a little general education and instruction in doctrine, the Bible and the work of a pastor.

From the very beginning the Ruanda Mission has sought to establish an indigenous Church, not dependent on foreign leadership, but ultimately modelled on Anglican lines. In achieving this, it followed the basic scheme planned for the Church of Uganda by that missionary statesman, Bishop Tucker. According to this, the area around each mission centre was divided into districts, over which was placed a senior evangelist and, in later years, an ordained pastor responsible for the network of small churches in the district, each with its own resident evangelist and local Christian Council. These referred their decisions to the Deanery Council, and in 1940 was formed the first Diocesan Council of the Church of Ruanda-Urundi, consisting of Africans and missionaries, and the rather more complicated framework was firmly in place.

The early system had its disadvantages, as has already been pointed out, but some of these early evangelists were heroes and heroines. Isolated and persecuted, they stuck to their posts, often teaching a creed they barely understood themselves.

Some, on the other hand, were shining, enlightened Christians. There were the teacher and his wife, who resolutely cut down the tree where the local god was supposed to live to show they did not fear the results, which included being childless, and a few months later they triumphantly carried in their first baby for christening and gave him the name Niyonzima (the Living God). Stefano, in charge of another church, was a rich man but he left all to follow Christ. Two good cows were offered him in an attempt to make him give up Christianity, but he answered, "The Son of God gave His life for me, and now I have Eternal Life and I shall go and be with Him."

"To stand for Jesus on the hills, you have to be right out for Him," wrote Joy Gerson. "Half measures are no good in the midst of such heathen darkness, and many of the village readers put us to shame. Sometimes they are beaten, but that does not stop them. At one of the most distant schools, we heard that one of their readers, a newly baptized lad of about seventeen, had just died and his death had done for that district more than any amount of teaching. When he was very ill he called his heathen parents and said, 'When I am gone you must not use my name in your heathen oaths, as you usually do when your children die; and you must not offer anything for my spirit because I am going to be alive, and not dead as you think.' And all this time he had real peace and no fear whatever. His death meant more than very many sermons."

The first central churches were built mainly with gifts from overseas, although from the outset this was a point of dissension, and Jim Brazier wrote in 1937: "After five years of worship in a grass shelter, and six months in the open, we have a nice building in burnt brick, with sanctuary and communion rails, to give dignity to our Sunday worship. Six years seems a long time to wait for a church, but I think the idea that the beginning of a missionary work must be the erection of a magnificent building is very questionable. The building should be one of the fruits of changed lives, not the prelude to them. Actually, ours is not, because all the expense was borne by a generous donor in England."

The first brick churches, given by friends from overseas, were put up as an offering to God and filled to overflowing; but the early buildings did not last for ever, and once again, when they needed repair and new ones were crying out to be built, God's clocks were keeping perfect time. By 1936, revival was already sweeping the land, and one of the most marked fruits was the surge of sacrificial giving. "They so loved that they gave." Only a few years later we read, "Self support is rising greatly. In 1941 it was 4,500 francs; in 1942, 9,000 francs and the idea of giving a tenth is growing. The other day a young boy sold a goat for 70 francs. He decided to give 7 francs to God, but later was tempted to give only four. In a meeting he confessed to his broken promise and brought the whole tenth."

It was those few missionaries who chose the hard, unpopular way of refusing to help financially or to launch appeals, who probably did most to force the infant Church to stand on its unsteady feet, and then to trust God. Paulo, the evangelist, brought a cow for God's work—the dowry for his future bride. People told him he was very foolish and suggested that he gave the less valuable bull, but his reply was typical of hundreds given over those years when the flame of love burned so brightly. "This is not a big thing, but a little one. The death of my Lord to redeem me is of great price; what I have given Him is equal to nothing."

By 1940 the whole idea had caught on and churches at three rural centres had been built without any overseas help. These churches, costing up to £100 each, usually built on the top of a hill commanding the whole district, are monuments to the love and labour of their congregations. At one, for months on end, everyone who came to pray on the site brought a brick in their hands; and even the little children were taught to bring small fistfuls of sweet corn as their offering to God. The buildings are mostly unadorned and unfurnished, apart from a communion table, and the people bring their own mats and sit on the floor. Far more beautiful than any device of stained glass are the rolling hills and valleys and open skies to be seen through the unglazed lancet windows and the ever-open door.

In the meantime some sort of Church framework was being erected. In 1935 when Arthur Pitt-Pitts accepted the position of Archdeacon and Field Secretary of the Ruanda Mission, he sought to unite these independent centres into a national Church under a single leadership. In 1937 this frail, humble man of God, just recovering from severe para-typhoid, started his new ecclesiastical headquarters at Buye in a thatched hut on a windy hill-top 6,300 feet above sea-level. Eleven brave evangelists pioneered the work with him.

After the death of Archdeacon Pitt-Pitts it was realized that the Field Secretaryship and care of the Church was too great a burden for one man, and Dr Stanley Smith became Field Secretary until 1957 when he handed over the leadership to Dr Godfrey Hindley. Harold Guillebaud fulfilled his brief ministry as Archdeacon and was succeeded by Jim Brazier.

All through these years the revival was working as a ferment in the Church and the new wine needed new wineskins; for the old tight framework was proving a real barrier to the outbreaking of God's Spirit. Indeed, the most bitter opponents of the spreading revival were often the Uganda church leaders themselves. It was humbling for a church leader to admit that he was cold, prejudiced, and lacked life and vision, and some feared the revival as they would the plague. Rules were issued in some places that no revivalist might preach in a church building. A split seemed inevitable, but it never came. The "pro-revival" section remained loyal. It was their church and what they longed for was its revival.

At Mukono Theological College the flame burned brightly. As student after student caught fire, strong in love and faith and zeal—though probably still weak in humility and tact—their daily fellowship meetings and bold criticism caused chaos in the College. They were ordered to conform to the recognized time-table and quieten down or leave, and twenty-five chose to leave, including William Nagenda. This may explain why some of East Africa's greatest spiritual leaders are unordained men. They spread over the length and breadth of the land and the churches received them with open arms and tears, while the College settled down again to its uninspired, conventional routine, only to find that it had become intolerable. Those who remained had seen Him, heard Him, known Him in the lives of these impossible young men who had left them, and soon they were crying to God that He would visit them afresh. And the Lord had mercy on their blind goodness and honest effort and the hard work done in His name, and poured out upon them a spirit of weeping, supplication and repentance that resulted in joy and salvation. Within a year or two a steady little stream of revived clergy were coming from the College to lead the churches all over the land.

No African was more used by God in building up the Church in Kigezi than Ezekieri Balaba who had been appointed Rural Dean in 1946 and succeeded Lawrence Barham as Archdeacon of Ankole and Kigezi in 1959. Joe Church wrote of him after his death in 1965: "I never remember Ezekieri being angry in over thirty years, nor do I ever remember a hard word in all our discussions and challenges together because Ezekieri always spoke with grace. Yet he was a very human man and had many testings with his large family of twelve children."

In Rwanda and Burundi the Protestant Alliance had convened the United Church Council in 1943 at Buye, with African delegates of every Mission bearing equal responsibility with the missionaries for the decisions made. This enabled the whole Protestant body of Rwanda and Burundi to think and act unitedly. It was a tremendous step forward.

Another step forward was in 1951. Jim Brazier was consecrated as the first Bishop for Kigezi, Rwanda and Burundi and made his headquarters at Buye. But it was not until 1956 that the first Burundi deacons were ordained as full pastors. It was an historic occasion and the group was photographed by the grave of Archdeacon Guillebaud, the one who first gave them the Word of God.

After that, things moved fast. "The Kenya, Uganda and Tanzania Churches," prophesied one in 1958, "still count as colonies of Canterbury, but the day is drawing near when that status will be changed to that of a self-governing province. For Uganda, it may come in 1960, and that will involve Rwanda and Burundi becoming a separate diocese under an Archbishop of Uganda." This actually happened on 1st July 1960, when C.M.S. Ruanda officially became *L'Eglise Anglicane du Ruanda-*

Urundi with a Diocesan Council as the directing authority and the direction of all primary schools in African hands.

It was a bleak time in Rwanda; a time when relations between missionary and national were as strained as they had ever been, and trust between Christians was at a low ebb. A Civil War involving the two main tribal groups, the Tutsi and the Hutu, was raging and the majority of Christians found it impossible to steer clear of politics. Many were forced into a warfare for which they had no sympathy and, being forced into it, performed deeds that clouded their consciences and hindered their fellowship with God and each other. Within the next two or three years, a number of loved leaders were to be taken from their midst: Pastor Yona, killed by terrorists; John Clayton, shot by robbers in his home at Buye; Pastor Timoteyo, struck by lightning in his church; John Sharp, dying in England; Pat Walker, killed in a car accident; Andrew Bowman, flown home suddenly for brain surgery and unable to return to the mission field for five years; and Dr Hindley and Dr Church, who had to leave the country for reasons of political safety.

All this hit so hard at the communities that it seemed impossible to carry on Buye Theological College at its full capacity, and senior students were sent up to Mukono College in Uganda. Rwanda had already provided for its own trainees by opening the Stanley Smith Theological College at Gahini in 1964 under the leadership of Canon Albert Brown.

Yet in spite of all this, 1965 was a year of historical significance in the development of the Church for it marked the election of Erica Sabiti as Archbishop of Uganda, Rwanda and Burundi; Yohana Nkunzumwani, Bishop of Burundi and Adoniya Subununguri, Bishop of Rwanda. Canon Ian Leakey and Canon Albert Brown were appointed as Bishops' advisers and two years later Richard Lyth, son-in-law of Dr Stanley Smith, was unanimously elected Bishop of Kigezi.

Would the complete handing over of authority be too difficult a matter to negotiate in a war-torn country, where the wounds and suspicions had barely begun to heal? And how far was the African Church ready to take complete control? What was the future role of the missionaries? Should they quietly withdraw over the next few years, or was there still a place for them? The atmosphere at the missionary conference in 1966 could have been rather tense, and it was probably the gracious, reassuring counsel of Erica Sabiti that did most to put everyone at their ease. He felt there was still a very great part to be played by missionaries who were willing to work under the direction of the African Church, but he warned them most earnestly of the deadly pitfall of handing over publicly, and then criticizing privately behind the backs of their leaders. This wise counsel was followed by a Bible reading by Dr Kenneth Buxton who, as Chairman of the Ruanda Council, had come on an official visit from England. He pointed out how Moses was criticized by fellow-workers, and the company with one accord began to pray. There was a spontaneous chain of short prayers offered up to God, and nearly all sought forgiveness for the sin of criticism. Outwardly, there was nothing much to show for the conference. Inwardly, a great step forward had been taken as the missionaries pledged themselves afresh to be loyal to the National Church and its leaders.

They soon found there was plenty for them to do. Spiritually the African leaders were ready to take over, but there were few trained to carry on outreach projects, or to man the educational and medical posts in the church schools and hospitals. And the African pastors still lacked the "standing" of the missionary. The Rwanda Church had never been officially recognized and had no *personalité civile* after Independence. Bert Osborn urged the Church to go to the appropriate government department to confer about the signing of the papers. "You have got it wrong," they replied. "This is not our African Church; this is the Church of God and you are in it, too. You must go to the Government because they know you and you have standing." Finally they decided to go as a team, black and white, not once, but many times, and the recognition was granted in 1964.

There was much to be done to train African laity to run the departments that have for so many years, in European countries, fed and enriched the central life of the Church. In 1965, Margaret Clayton came down from Uganda and the first leaders' conference of the Mothers' Union took place in Rwanda when fourteen women gathered from all over the country. This work had been started, in a small way, by Mrs Barham, but now with Mrs Sebununguri, the Bishop's wife, as President, it was spreading all over the country. Doreen Peck, Mrs Albert Brown, Nina Putman and others, had been tireless in promoting its welfare both in Rwanda and Burundi. Bible study outlines were prepared and sent out to leaders; hygiene, cooking, dressmaking, child care and dietetics were taught in many a house, prayer hut or sheltered garden, and the whole standard of the rural Christian homes was improving. In 1966, sixty women and many babies gathered for their second leaders' conference at Gahini.

Bishop Lyth had aimed at answering the criticism so often levelled at the Church in recent years. "It is so spiritual that it fails to tackle the real problems of the world." He launched Christian Rural Service which later spread throughout Uganda. It is a project that recognizes man as an entity of body, soul and spirit, for Christ made it clear that He cared for the whole man. Nora Lyth wrote: "C.R.S. is not just another social service, but an arm of the Church for reaching out with the love and concern of God for the whole of men's lives, drawing them to know Him."

So Bishop Lyth began to train men and to send them out into the villages. "As the initial period of training in the classroom and in the field was completed," he wrote, "and as the people of the district came to realize what we were here for and began to call for us to come and help them, we divided the team up into pairs (like our Lord's disciples) and one pair went to live and work in each county of the district. As over 60 per cent of the men and 80 per cent of the women of the district are unable to read and write, one of the early tasks that the field workers threw themselves into was the formation of adult literacy classes and the training of volunteer teachers for these. The publication of the whole Bible for the first time in the local language was an added incentive to these classes, and the field workers had many opportunities for teaching about the Lord. Our field workers have formed a number of self-help groups of farmers who have united for the purpose of benefiting their community. They have created protected springs for the villagers instead of their having to use swamp water; sometimes they have constructed a road where none existed before, so that more villages can be served by motor transport. Women have been taught how to make smokeless kitchens at no cost except the hard work of digging and moulding clay for stoves and chimneys. The results could be tremendous. No more babies falling into the fire; no more infected eyes from hours spent in an atmosphere of thick smoke."

In Rwanda David Weston taught the local people to improve their standard of living through agriculture, and the response was great. Later James Brown at Maranyundo offered help with bee and poultry keeping, cattle improvement, vegetable growing, water supply, literacy and health instruction. Men realized the love of Christ through people who really cared and this was right, for He bore not only their sins, but all the griefs that spring from sin—hunger, poverty, famine and war. So the Church should become a home to which men turn in all their problems and find sympathy, healing and practical help.

Youth work within the Church offered another field of opportunity. Norma Westlake, Pat Brooks, Viera Gray and others, started Boys' and Girls' Brigades and trained leaders. Doreen Sharp carried on the work, so dear to her husband, of the Christian Union Branches in schools, and the Kitleys travelled round the schools of Burundi encouraging Inter-School Christian Fellowships. Pat and Pam Brooks developed work among students in Burundi's capital, Bujumbura, where Dorothée de Benoit had joined the staff of Radio Cordac, the Christian broadcasting station.

At Kigali, Rwanda's rapidly expanding capital, a large site was given to the Anglican Church. The first building of any size to be erected on it was a hall to be used, not only for services till the cathedral was finished, but as a youth centre for the many young people who were being contacted daily.

So, "Like a mighty army moves the Church of God," but the generals are now the Africans and the missionaries move with the rank and file.

"My people were pagans," said the Bishop of Rwanda, "and I never knew my father. I worked with missionaries as a house-boy, but one day a Voice said to me, 'Give back what you stole.' So I repented and was forgiven. After many years of teaching and training the Lord made me a bishop and I was afraid and said, 'What can I do? How can I do it aright?' Then Bishop Barham said to me, 'If you continue to walk with Jesus and be a humble man, you can do it. If you are proud and stubborn and trust in being a bishop, then it will be hard.' So far, He gives me grace to keep repenting. To me, the happiest day of my life is not the day that I became a bishop, but the day I came to know Jesus."

18

The Church in the Fire

Worldly ambition, materialism, love of money, are the enemies of any Church in any age and, in the 1950's, the Church in Rwanda felt their full impact. The church schools were the key to promotion and western "civilization". The gold remained and shone brightly, but it was more and more mixed with dross. Perhaps it was for that reason that from 1959–62 God allowed His Church to pass through a fire of testing and persecution, so all that was base was shrivelled, and all that was true was refined and purified.

To understand the tragedy of those years it is necessary to know something of the hitherto accepted social system of Rwanda. The present population density is the result of two waves of conquest. The original inhabitants of Rwanda are thought to have been a pygmy people known as the Twa who were mostly hunters and potters. In 1960 they constituted less than 1 per cent of the population.

The first conquerors were an agricultural Bantu people known as Hutu, who are characterized by woolly hair, flat broad noses, thick lips and middle stature. They began by conquering the forest and clearing the bush with their hoes. In 1960 they constituted 85 per cent of Rwanda's three million people.

Several centuries ago a tall, slender, haughty, aristocratic people known as the Tutsi began the second conquest of Rwanda. Reputed to have come from Ethiopia or the Nile Valley, the Tutsi were the outer fringe of a great south-bound pastoral migration. They constitute less than 15 per cent of the population of Rwanda, and the Tutsi conquest of Rwanda and the Hutu was achieved through a combination of persuasion and force. The highly-organized Tutsi, who subsist mainly on their cattle which they value above everything else, entered the country under the banner of their king, known as the Mwami, whose army was made up of a series of warrior groups under military lords. They negotiated with individual Hutu clan chiefs to provide protection for the clans in exchange for the Hutu accepting the Tutsi lords as their patrons. Where the Hutu chiefs resisted, they were defeated by the superior military organization and resources of the Tutsi. In the end a working compromise was reached, and the Hutu entered into a contract with the Tutsi lords in order to obtain cattle and protection, and they provided the Tutsi lords in exchange with free labour, gifts, personal service and foodstuffs.

This feudal system flourished for many years in both Rwanda and Burundi, based on the belief in the inherent inequality of human beings. According to legend, the first King of Rwanda had three sons, Gatutsi, Gahutu and Gatwa. When nearing his death, he gave each of his sons a pot of milk to guard overnight. Gatutsi faithfully stayed awake to guard the pot and returned it to his father full next day. Gahutu dozed off and let the pot spill and returned it half empty. The greedy Gatwa guzzled down the milk and came back empty-handed. Therefore the King chose Gatutsi as his successor, to be for ever exempt from manual labour, making Gahutu his serf, while Gatwa was banished from the human world.

When the Belgian forces occupied Rwanda in 1916, after a short period of German rule, they made no attempt, at first, to curb the power of the Mwami and his Tutsi chiefs. On the contrary, they confined their education and government posts to the Tutsi élite. But over the years, clashes occurred and the power of the Tutsi chiefs gradually lessened. In 1956 a National Council of Rwanda was created, whose membership was firmly controlled by colonial Government.

The Church in the Fire

But the Hutu were being educated too, and ideals of democracy and equal rights were beginning to penetrate, while the memories of oppressions rankled furiously. "When will we regularize our injustices?" asked a Hutu poet in one of the current literary works, and the answer was, "When the Hutu no longer has the soul of a serf. For that, he must be reborn."

In 1960 Independence came to the Congo. Rwanda realized that the Belgians might not stay for ever, and both Tutsi and Hutu began to prepare for the inevitable clash. In September 1959 a new political party was formed, the PARMEHUTU (*Parti d'Emancipation des Hutus*). On 24th July 1959 the forty-six-year-old Mwami died suddenly and mysteriously, without having nominated a successor. The Tutsis immediately chose his nephew as the new King and the Belgians acquiesced. A few brutal assassinations of leading Hutu occurred, and then the volcano erupted. For the first time in history, the Hutu rose *en masse* against their feudal lords. The new Mwami fled to Burundi and the country started its full-scale civil war.

An effort to solve these troubles by a general election resulted in a 71 per cent vote in favour of the Hutu parties. Riots, bloodshed and massacre continued in waves, until Independence was granted under the wise, dedicated rule of President Kayibanda on 1st July 1962, and Rwanda and Burundi became separate states.

The horror that was to become so widespread started with a small fight near Shyogwe, in October 1959, and soon Peter and Elisabeth Guillebaud, Mabel Jones and others there found themselves in the centre of war and terror. Men with axes were sweeping over the hills, cutting down banana and coffee plantations, burning the Tutsi huts, killing the cattle. The missionaries had to make up their minds whether they would be involved in what was, basically, a major political issue or not. To remain neutral would be to condone the murder of hundreds. They decided to open their doors to the refugees.

First to arrive was a Christian teacher, terrified and weeping,

201

begging Peter to rescue his wife and children. That was the first of many hazardous journeys over roads and up hill-sides garrisoned with armed, drunken troops to rescue those who were in danger of death. Peter wrote vividly to his son about these days.

"Thursday, 5th November. This is a day on which we seemed to pass the point of no return. In the morning the grim, blood-curdling cries began about 9 a.m. Suddenly, down the hill and across our site came pouring a motley host of hundreds of men and boys, shrieking and dancing, waving knives and spears, bashing in the doors and pulling the tiles off the roofs of the houses in their way. They went on to the chief's house and the dispenser's house, destroying them both utterly. Bombs weren't in it! All we could do was to go out in the evening and pick up the families and fix them up in our house with Rosemary and Dorothée.

"Friday, 6th November. Rumours are rife that it is our turn to be attacked because we have sheltered the refugees. We went to rescue a judge's wife whose leg had been broken, and on the way back we met a huge band (over 100) armed to the teeth. It was an alarming experience to pass between the divided ranks, glaring at us in silence. We now have to accommodate the judge's wife and children.

"Sunday, 8th November. Good time in church, but how our people need to see the Lord and escape from that vicious trio of sins—fear, hate and rumour-mongering. Our spiritual need is very great and it is pathetic to see responsible people crumple up and become like children. During church, a government official arrived in a Jeep with a telegram proclaiming martial law and a curfew, and later a band of wild men came down the road beating drums and yelling to try and rouse people, but people won't respond any more. Panic is giving way to black, black despair as we see the ruin of this country."

But in the midst of all the chaos and ruin, people in the district began to flee in one direction—up the hill to the mission

houses and to the church and pastorate at Hanika, which was
fast becoming a recognized refugee centre. A man was chased by
an armed gang and ran for half a mile with one of his enemies
brandishing a knife behind him. As he flung himself over the
mission boundary, his enemy stopped and called to him,
"You're all right now, aren't you? You've reached *Iman'
ishimwe* (Praise the Lord)." "To come here is like coming into
Heaven when you compare it with prevailing relationships on
our stations, or anywhere else in the country," said a Roman
Catholic priest. "You people are unlike any others these days,"
said another who came to them for help.

Adversity was drawing them together, spiritually as well as
physically. By 12th November, there were three hundred homeless people sheltering on the mission grounds, and it was then
that Mabel Jones, who was coping with the terrified schoolchildren, made a large copy of a picture that was to become the
symbol of safety to many throughout the riots. It was a picture
of a pack of ravenous wolves howling at two sheep, a black and
a white one, but a pierced hand held back the hungry beasts
and the sheep were safe behind that barrier. As yet too dazed
and broken-hearted by loss and bereavement, there was no
great spiritual response at first, but their guests knew that,
temporarily at least, they were safe and could stop running
away.

"Why do you come here?" asked a Christian, who found his
house so full that he could barely enter it himself. "Don't you
see my house is grass and thatched like your own? Why should
you think that you are safer here?"

"Because we know that you have no enemies," they replied.

And while many Christians were broken and dazed by the
loss of all their earthly goods, others stood firm and fixed their
eyes steadfastly on the things that are eternal. An old man was
warned that a gang was coming his way, so he quietly went out
to meet them and stood in front of his hut. "What have you
come for?" he asked. "We have come to burn your house,"

they replied. He stood aside. "That's only wood and grass," he said, "you can burn that if you like, but I have something you can't burn and that is my home in Heaven which Jesus has gone to prepare for me."

Another was found quietly praising God after his new house had been razed to the ground. "I never thought anything would happen to my house, but when I saw the ruins, the Lord gave me peace. I brought nothing into this world, and I can take nothing out of it. No one can take away my eternal life and my home in Heaven."

Another Tutsi had lost his cows, his home and all his possessions. "You Europeans", he said, "may not think much of the loss of a cow, but to us it is like losing a child. I have chronic indigestion and I always drink milk. I thought if I ever lost my cows I would be finished, but since all this I have had no indigestion for the Lord has satisfied me."

At Shyira in the north, Doreen Peck and Josephine Stancliffe were in the same predicament. How deeply should they get involved? Should they take sides or not? And once again the question was decided for them. On 4th November, they noticed columns of smoke rising here and there over the beautiful countryside and gradually drawing nearer. Next day, they could see the glow of flames and burning roofs all over the hillside below them and then the refugees began to arrive. By next morning there were about three hundred Tutsi lodging in every corner of the house and hospital, and rumours were spreading like wildfire that Shyira hill was the next point of attack as several Tutsi, wanted by the bands, were there in hiding— although the missionaries had refused to shelter the district chief and his family, feeling that this constituted almost certain massacre for all the rest. The burning houses and plantations now formed a complete ring of fire and smoke round the premises and at 3 p.m. an emergency meeting of church leaders was called. They decided that Josephine, the local evangelist, and the hospital dresser were to drive to Gahini and get help, and Doreen Peck was to stay with the people and face up to whatever might come.

So Josephine set out on her epic journey through the seared, burning countryside and on through the blackness of the night, passing heavily-armed gangs on the road, but she mostly remembers the sense of peace ("My peace I leave with you") and she reached her one-hundred-and-twenty-mile destination in safety and arrived back late the following night with Ted Sisley and their own pastor, who had been on holiday.

Doreen Peck, now the only missionary on the place, was also conscious of that amazing peace. After Josephine had left, armed raiders blowing horns rushed across the mission property; and the fires were very near. There was plenty to do trying to provide food for her three hundred terrified guests, but at last they were all huddled down, some fitfully sleeping. She opened *Daily Light* and the old words seemed written afresh for her alone on that evening in November. "The children of Israel pitched before them like two little flocks of kids, but the Syrians filled the country. I will deliver this great multitude into thy hand, and ye shall know that I am the Lord. They shall fight against thee, but they shall not prevail against thee, for I am with thee." She lay down and slept and woke at 3 a.m. clear and certain of her guidance. They had done wrong in refusing to shelter the chief and his family. The verse "Greater love hath no man than this, that a man lay down his life for his friends," was ringing in her ears, and she got up at once and went out into the inky night to rouse the chief's family and fetch them in. It was now Sunday, and very soon the stiff, huddled forms awoke and the morning mists blended with the smoke of the burnings, very, very near now. They all gathered for their Sunday morning service as usual, and committed themselves to God.

At midday the message came. A great band of soldiers armed with spears and staves were standing on the border of the mission premises and wished to see the missionary in charge, so Doreen and the evangelist's wife walked down the hill to talk to them. A hush fell over them and they listened in shamed amazement as she assured them that she had no interest in parties or politics. She was there to tell all men about the love of God and Christ's death for all. Politely but firmly they explained that that was all very well, but she was harbouring their enemies and interfering with official orders. Certain people must be given up altogether, and the headmaster, a Hutu, must be produced, as he was said to be missing and it was suspected that he had been murdered by the Tutsi. Unless he appeared alive within two hours, they would attack the Mission, capture the refugees and burn their houses.

It was then that the voice that answered seemed to Doreen to belong to someone else altogether. Amazed, unafraid, she found herself saying, "You cannot come up this hill. It is God's hill." A young lad, his eyes blazing with hate, thrust his face close to hers and shouted, "There is no God, Mademoiselle." "Oh yes, there is," she replied. "And you will see that He is going to protect this hill from harm."

There was an angry muttering and a move was made to rush past her up the hill, but the pierced hand was stretched out in protection round that frail flock and the bandits hung back. Doreen and Edreda climbed the hill alone. But Doreen was in a very difficult position, for the schoolmaster *had* disappeared and no one could tell of his whereabouts. Time was passing and dusk was falling. She gathered the crowd and warned them of the impending danger and advised as many as possible to try and slip away in the dark. But before they went they prayed together and even as they prayed the rain began coming down in torrents. Mass attack through the liquid mud of Shyira hill would be virtually impossible and some began singing songs of praise and joy. Nobody saw God's invisible hosts, the horses and chariots of fire round about the hill, but they were certainly there.

Another messenger arrived through the rain. News of the

whereabouts of the headmaster must be produced before midnight or the attack would take place at 7 a.m. Doreen sat down to answer the letter and while she was still writing, another messenger came in with a note. It was from the missing schoolmaster himself, safe, but in hiding. She sent off copies of the letter to the raiders and just as the messenger was leaving a car chugged up the hill.

Josephine, Ted Sisley and their own pastor were back with a written promise of protection and the power to call on military aid if necessary.

"We praised the Lord, who had delivered us when there seemed no possible escape for our property and perhaps for the lives of some," wrote Doreen. "Early in the evening, as I faced the possible loss of all my goods, I knew that nothing must ever matter again except to preach the Lord Jesus in His saving power and to bow to His will in all things."

But, in spite of military protection, the hospital was constantly threatened and, with three hundred people in residence, its real task of caring for the sick became impossible. When Dr Adeney arrived two days later, he consulted with the Administrator about moving the refugees to safety. The Uganda Government had announced that they would accept unarmed refugees, and transport was provided to take them north over the Uganda border.

It was a sad, busy night as the crowd faced the prospect of leaving their homes and country, perhaps for ever. Seven lorries arrived early in the morning and the whole three hundred were borne downhill into the thick, white, valley mists, over the rolling countryside and black tracks of Rwanda to the Kigezi border where they were going. What they would find was uncertain. Dr Adeney left the convoy to turn aside at one point to see whether two Tutsi girls who lived at another pastorate were safe; and there he found the one man who could help them, Kosiya Shalita who was now an Assistant Bishop in Uganda. The Bishop set off immediately "to prepare a place for them" at the first Protestant centre inside Uganda. So when, after three hours of anxious waiting at the frontier, the lorries trundled into safety, the tide of refugees found everything ready for their reception.

Kigeme and Gahini escaped bloodshed at the beginning of the riots and, at Gahini at least, this was probably due to the gathering that took place by moonlight under the trees on 8th November 1959, when the Protestant sub-chiefs and leaders of the African Church met to discuss what action they should take. Unanimously, they asked Dr Church to request the Administrator not to send Congolese soldiers to protect the hill. When asked why, they said they were more afraid of the Congolese soldiers than of the Hutu rioters and preferred to let God look after them, and in spite of fears and numerous suspicions, there were no real incidents for nearly two years. Like all the other mission centres, they sheltered homeless, starving Tutsi in danger of massacre. For five months they gave refuge to the Queen Mother, and finally transported her over the border into Uganda.

Then the blow fell. In August 1961 the British Consul advised Dr Joe Church to leave the country. Owing to his services to the Tutsi he had, over the months, become a marked man and his safety could no longer be guaranteed. Although his son, John, with his wife Rhoda, had come to replace him medically, it was a bitter blow for the African Church at that critical hour. Only a fortnight later terror broke loose at Gahini.

Many are the ineffaceable memories of those days. Janet Smith, the sister in charge of the hospital, remembers driving the Sisley children to safety through the burning kraals and plantations; going out into the smouldering countryside to bring in the old, the homeless and the wounded; the sorrow of the old pastor, whose precious Bible was destroyed; the crowds arriving with their cattle. Each night lorries arrived to convey people, at a high price, over the Uganda frontier, but they left their cows and dogs behind them, and soon the grass was ex-

hausted. Cows began to die all over the mission hill and the
flies came; then rabies broke out and four victims died of hydro-
phobia before the doctor shot twenty-four dogs. She remembers
working all night by torchlight to help save seven people
whose heads had been partly severed with hoes while they were
trying to hide in a banana patch. Only one survived.

"This is the saddest letter I could ever have to write to you.
. . . It came like a whirlwind today," wrote Dr John Church,
left in charge. "While I was doing the ward round, a tall Tutsi
rushed into the ward and besought me to save him. He was
followed by a gang of Hutu. I drove them out and took the
man into the prayer room while a huge crowd collected outside. I refused to allow them to enter, but later Belgian soldiers
came and took the poor man away. By afternoon the whole
countryside was ablaze and the refugees began pouring in. We
had a good time at the fellowship meeting, just crying to the
Lord to save us. Then we went out in three cars and brought
in all the women and children we could find. . . . News came
that Timoteyo, our pastor, had been attacked. Ted Sisley went
right through the burnings to Timoteyo's house and met him
being carried out, speared through the upper thigh. Then they
came down this side of the hill and burned out our next-door
neighbour and he has been beaten up and one ear is hanging.
. . . It is now midnight and from my window I can count seven
kraals burning. The gang has said if any of us missionaries are
seen off the mission hill we shall be killed. We don't mind
these threats because the Lord is with us, but we are only going
out to save lives."

In the Church things were as low as they could be spiritually.
Most people were intimidated by terror and distrust and the
fires of revival that had burned so brightly seemed, for a time,
almost extinguished. Yet, here and there, shining lights refused
to be dimmed, and right from the midst of it all Joe Church
received the following letter from one who had been cruelly
beaten and nearly blinded:

"We are all well because Jesus has turned death into victory through the wonderful Gospel you brought to us. You know all that has happened to us in Rwanda. Here, we have had our home destroyed, and after it happened I was beaten for four days and left for dead. But this time was a blessing to my soul. All the time they were beating me, I couldn't help singing and saying, over and over again, 'Jesus be praised.' I kept praying for them very much all the time, and in my heart I was thankful because they said they had nothing against me except the fact that I was a Tutsi.

"Now, in case we shall never meet again before I die, I want to tell you that you and the other missionaries who brought the Gospel to us have done a great work. When I think how you found me in those days, I love you more than you know. Only Jesus knows how much I love you. I know quite well that you did not come for any personal gain or for what you could make out of it, so I want to comfort you in all suffering that may come to you 'even unto death' not to be downhearted; it is not in vain. Jesus will give you your reward. It is I, A. Mandari (Gahini, 2.3.62)."

It was a bitter experience for missionaries all over Rwanda to see many in whom they had trusted sink rapidly through fear, into intrigue, hatred and bloodshed, but the few who stood firm came through shining and purified and strengthened in love. To them, a letter written by Festo Kivengere to the Rwanda Church at the outbreak of war, containing the following extract, came as a trumpet call:

"The news of your troubles reached us while we were conducting an evangelistic mission in Tanzania. Our hearts went out to you in prayer and the strain of our prayer was in the words of our Lord, 'I do not ask that Thou wilt take them out of the world (or out of Rwanda) but that Thou wilt keep them from the evil.' A special message comes from our brother Heshbon Mwangi from Kikuyu in the name of the Kikuyu brethren in Kenya. He suffered much for Jesus Christ in the

Mau-Mau rebellion, and he says to the brethren in Rwanda,
'Keep a positive testimony in word and deed. Use only one
weapon, that of Calvary love for all, particularly those that are
persecuting you.' It was that positive, fearless testimony of love
which never valued life more than the witness of Jesus, that
won the day in Kikuyu."

Won for us at great cost, fearful to grasp, and yet invincible
when rightly wielded, the weapon of Calvary love alone truly
triumphed. Witness a senior African overseer coming in to take
morning prayers for the workmen on the mission hill. During
the night his own house and his mother-in-law's and his whole
store of winter grain had been burnt, yet he does not appear
much shaken or upset. "Dear Lord," he prays, "please follow
those who set fire to our house and help them to repent and
follow Thee." Then turning to the gathered company, he said,
"I do not know who lit those fires in the night. Although I
have lost a house, furniture and much of our food for the next
three months, I want you to know that I forgive whoever did
it just as my Lord Jesus forgave me. My only longing is that
these men may turn to Jesus in repentance."

Here is a woman turning back to the charred remains of her
little home. The flames have died down as she kneels among
the ashes and prays. She is praying for those who have burnt
her out, and committing her blank future to God; the journey,
empty-handed, to the nearest border; the poverty in the refugee
camp and the uncertainty.

> *Peace, perfect peace; our future all unknown,*
> *Jesus we know, and He is on the Throne.*

Christmas communion service in Shyira church—a large congregation had come from all over the ravaged, war-scarred
area to celebrate the song of the angels, "Unto you is born a
Saviour. Peace and goodwill to men." Sitting in the congregation are two ladies, the mother and aunt of the outstanding
Protestant member of Parliament, who had just been murdered

when travelling in his car by night. As the familiar words rang through the church, "Ye that do truly and earnestly repent of your sins and are in love and charity with your neighbours, draw near with faith and take this Holy Sacrament," the quiet forward movement of the worshippers was checked by the sound of bitter weeping. The two bereaved ladies could not draw near. So the service was interrupted, while in sight of the symbols of the Lord's love and sacrifice, they sobbed out their hatred and thoughts of revenge and found forgiveness through the broken Body and the Blood of Christ. And the great revival chorus rose quietly from the worshippers:

Glory, glory, Hallelujah,
Glory, glory to the Lamb,
Oh, the cleansing Blood has reached me,
Glory, glory to the Lamb.

A schoolmaster is lying on the ground, with a bullet through his chest, horribly mutilated with a panga (a sharp knife for cutting firewood). His blood is flowing fast, but he can still gasp out a few words. "I have done nothing wrong. I am not in any party because I am a saved man. I do not hate anyone. I am not afraid to die because I shall go to my heavenly home. . . ."

A nurse at Gahini is leaning over an old man, wantonly attacked, dying of terrible head and neck wounds. He is whispering something, a last message, *"Nta kindi keretse Yesu"* (There is nothing else but Jesus).

The formation of the new Hutu Government technically brought the war to a close, but it left a land torn, divided, impoverished and broken-hearted. It left Christians whose consciences could never altogether let them rest again and a whole wake of hatred, suspicion and broken loyalties that took years to mend; wounds that will never, in this generation, quite heal. Yet in many of the apparently broken-down churches, God kept His people to do their work of rebuilding. The house of a

The Church in the Fire

Tutsi pastor stood on the hill-side, overlooking beautiful Lake Kivu, and was three times surrounded by Hutu raiders. Twice the local Hutu persuaded them to go away, telling them that this was a man of God, who loved everybody and must not be harmed; but the third time the raiders came at night, forced their way into his home and smashed his lamp. Standing in the dark, he asked them gently why they had come. They had no answer to that question and went away ashamed.

Speaking of those difficult times, he said, "When I look out on Lake Kivu I often see great storms. Rain and cloud blot out the islands. It seems as though they have disappeared as a result of the fury of the elements, but the wind blows the clouds away and we see the islands again, greener and more beautiful than ever as a result of the storm. Why are they not overthrown or destroyed? It is because they are founded on the rock and remain firm. Our work for the Lord is like that. It seems it must be overthrown by the testings of these difficult times, but it is founded on the Lord Jesus Himself, and He cannot be overthrown."

So the tempest passed, submerging and uprooting all that was built on sand and all that had trusted in man. But the true, revived Church, founded on Christ, rooted and grounded in love, shone out fairer and greener than ever before. The "one weapon" had triumphed.

19

Refugees

Simultaneously with the riots there appeared in Rwanda itself, and in all the neighbouring countries, a totally new mission field—the refugee camp.

Yet at least some of those who became leading workers among the refugees had had some previous experience. Dr and Mrs Hindley, who were both in England when the riots broke out, had lived through the famine at Shyira in the forties and sheltered six to seven hundred starving victims. That year had always lived on in their memories as a special time when in a wonderful way they had worked as a team with the Christians at Shyira. They had formed themselves into little groups and, after a heavy day's work in the school or hospital, they would go straight off to help the famine victims. One group would kill a cow; another group would cook it, and so on, and late in the evening, six thousand feet up under those tremendous starry heavens, all would gather round the great camp fire which the refugees would light, and listen to the Gospel story. No one ever seemed tired, and one night when the great company, all saved from slow, agonizing death, had been listening in rapt attention to the words of life, the children broke out spontaneously into their favourite hymn:

> *There is no love like the love of Jesus,*
> *Never to fade or fall . . .*

Many found the Saviour and when, some thirteen years later, the great mass exodus over the borders began, Dr Hindley, who was then the Mission Field Secretary, remembered and realized the possibilities.

But Peter and Elisabeth Guillebaud and Alan Lindsay, camping in tents at Nyanza with six thousand hopeless, homeless refugees, had had no previous experience. Very little government help was forthcoming to begin with, and they had little with which to meet the invasion except their own amazing courage and faith in God. Peter's long letters to his son in England give vivid pictures of the conditions that prevailed, and the earliest ones show how near he himself was to panic and despair.

"15.10.61. Life is full of utter impossibilities and growing, yet insoluble, problems. Refugees are becoming more and more numerous—at least six thousand now. Think what it means to feed them, to ward off dysentery and typhoid in the most primitive conditions, without mentioning protecting them from attack. The Government has no plans whatever for evacuating, and hopes of getting them re-integrated become increasingly remote. What can we be heading for, but wholesale massacre?

"22.10.61. I am writing this in a tent by safari lamp in a waterlogged patch of grass (it *pelts* with rain!). We are living in conditions bordering on complete chaos. The Parmehutu are burning and destroying all round us and refugees are once again pouring in. We are completely swamped. We can't hope to fit them in. Men fight for one or two square feet in the church and I was hit just now, trying to separate a couple fighting in a place reserved for women. The pastor and others spend hours each evening trying to find space for at least the women and children. Hundreds of others crowd into a veritable town of grass hovels that leak like sieves in the terrible rain. There is a friendly, sympathetic Belgian given the job of advising over refugees and he could not be more helpful—except that he has nothing to help them with!"

At first the missionaries stood alone between the six

thousand and the rumbling threats and accusations that ringed them round, day and night, and sometimes one or another was literally alone. Peter was away pleading for government help on the day that Misaki, the pastor, was falsely accused and threatened. "I did not know what decision to take," wrote Mrs Guillebaud. "So I went with Misaki to conduct him out of town, leaving all the refugees to be protected by the angels." But by the beginning of November, faith, prayer and courage had prevailed and even in those ghastly surroundings, under daily fear of death or mutilation, the protecting hand of God was again beginning to be evident.

"Now we have sufficient food for all," wrote Peter, "but imagine trying to store food for six thousand in a tiny little storeroom 6 by 9 feet in the pastor's house. Then again in spite of hopelessly inadequate sanitation, we have had no typhoid and very little dysentery, although a lot of pneumonia and measles. All the way through we have been marvellously protected from attack. Again and again, police came to arrest refugees on dubious charges, but they never seemed able to find the people they were after. Above all, we praise God for the high morale and cheerfulness of the refugees. They seem to understand that they are on God's Hill. At night we hear groups singing hymns out in the cold mud, and if someone starts a quarrel or uses abusive language, others at once reprove him, saying, 'You must not talk like that on God's Hill.' Spiritually, it is a wonderful opportunity and we have had wonderful times telling about the Saviour who forgives and sets free from the curse of sin and hatred, showing us our own sin and not other people's. . . . To most, the Gospel is utterly new."

This camp was eventually ordered to disperse, and the borders were opened and the people flooded over into safety, until only the tracts of mud and the battered settlements remained—and the memories. Going round at night, dropping blankets on the most needy, the old and the little children; the crowds, the smell; working out the food, so many beans, so much maize flour, dried milk for babies and the aged; getting round the cheating and stealing—the children passed from family to family to increase the food ration; the dread of leaving the tent in the morning to face the insuperable problems— families separated, relatives lost; going out on the hills to rescue those in danger and meeting hostile bands as they carried the wounded to the car; visiting a pygmy woman, about to give birth on the mud floor of a crowded hut; watching a chief's wife bent double with hunger pains, with a baby at her breast . . . her husband had been killed some days before. The pastor's wife smuggled her secretly into her house and shared her own little supply of rice with her. . . .

And other memories, memories of God's guidance and protecting care so that the one who had written at the outset, "Life is full of utter impossibilities and growing, yet insoluble, problems," could write at the end:

> *He will pilot you and me*
> *O'er this rock-strewn, stormy sea,*
> *Trace His wounded feet's impress*
> *Through the trackless wilderness.*
> *You, who from the pit He drew,*
> *He will make a way for you.*

About sixty thousand refugees, many with nothing but the rags they stood up in, poured into Burundi, and both Buye and Buhiga were submerged. Buye was only fifteen miles over the border, and there were up to fifteen thousand squatting on the mission hill. The Hindleys worked indefatigably, distributing food, organizing primary schools and fighting disease. There were little groups of children under every tree, being taught as well as the lack of equipment would allow. Crowds sat in the Hindleys' garden just because it was a safe place to sit, silent and hopeless, doing nothing and asking nothing. At night, every building was crammed with women and children sleeping cheek by jowl, and night after night the missionaries crept round the sleeping forms with a limited number of sacks and woollen blankets with which to cover any child who had nothing over it at all.

Later, the place became a government food distribution area, with Oxfam, the Red Cross, and the World Council of Churches all sending help, and for four to five years Dr Hindley worked with these movements. But before all this was properly organized, there was one night when the missionaries had nothing to give at all, except the Word of life, and their faith was deeply tested. Was the Word strong enough to stand in its own right? Had they the faith to claim that the promises of God were true and could meet the present need of that evening —the need of the starving multitude? "We have nothing for you," they said simply, "but if you will believe, God will provide."

They were just finishing the preaching when they heard the sound of lorries chugging up the hill. They had come through from the Congo and they were loaded with food. None went hungry that night, and many, many in their suffering and poverty turned to the Lord. One day at Buye three hundred were baptized, most of them refugees who had found a refuge in Christ.

The doctors were rushed off their feet as disease was rife in the camps, and medical supplies ran out fast and could not be immediately replaced. Dr Hindley went up to Nyamata, the refugee camp in Rwanda, once a week and one night he arrived home with a little famine skeleton called Mose, whose plight was so pitiful that the doctor, who had six children of his own, just could not leave him behind.

The camp in Nyamata had been started in 1959 in a low-lying, sparsely-populated tract of land known as the Bugesera, a vast area of bush and scrub which extends westward into Tanzania. It is a land of long grass and thorny acacias, surrounded on three sides by crocodile-infested rivers and papyrus swamps. It was once a kingdom in its own right and its nomadic inhabitants still have customs and superstitions unknown to the rest of the land. Buffaloes and elephants were plentiful and tsetse fly and mosquito were rife in the swamps. It became a country to be feared, a shelter where criminals and fugitives fled and the original population dwindled.

In the mid-fifties the Belgian Government launched a campaign to drain the marshes and clear the tsetse fly, and an agricultural station was started. But the people needed to exploit the potentialities of this wilderness were lacking until 1959, when convoys of lorries crossed the river and unloaded their cargoes; thousands of terrified, dazed refugees and loads of grain. It could have ended in disaster, but a young Belgian Administrator, Monsieur Triplot, headed a team of volunteers from the Catholic and Protestant Missions, whose work it was to develop the new colony, and finally a wonderful job was done. Roads were built, plots were marked out for each family, houses were built, crops were planted.

But this took time. All that could be done to begin with was to crowd the refugees into temporary clearing shelters; row upon row of long corrugated iron sheds, where hundreds of families huddled in hopeless poverty and squalor. The nights were damp and the sheds leaked; the days were intolerably hot and the iron huts were like ovens. Epidemics of typhoid and dysentery broke out, and the mental suffering was a gnawing agony. Why should they be denied justice, they muttered, and be settled in this hot, shadeless land to be killed by lions and sleeping sickness? The prevailing mood was one of sullen despair or bitter anger, and even true Christians seemed to band together with the rest in passive resistance to all that the Government sought to do.

Here, perhaps more than in any other part, the weapon of Calvary love triumphed. Only a mile from Nyamata was the little mission out-school of Maranyundo, founded in 1935 when Joe Church, Yosiya Kinuka and Blasio Kigozi had taken a team to the Bugesera and left a carpenter behind in that lonely, fever-ridden death-trap. Yet the outpost had survived and in 1959 a Christian, named James, was a kind of lay pastor over the district. But when the refugees arrived, he was away working for his church certificate at Buye College, and his wife was holding the fort alone.

Dora Skipper, retired in Kampala and now in her sixties, heard of the situation and lost no time. She dug out her old safari clothes of the 1930's, procured a tent and a bicycle and set off. She lodged with the pastor's wife and cycled to the camp daily, getting to know the refugees, tracing lost relations, tending the sick, teaching the children, demonstrating and preaching the love of God. The discouraged Christians rallied round her and hope and faith were reborn. Many repented of despair and hatred, and began looking round to see what they could do for others.

But Miss Skipper had other commitments and could only stay a few weeks, and when they heard this the refugees were broken-hearted. They had felt that one ray of light and hope had dawned on their darkness and now even that was to be withdrawn. Many were ready to follow, but they needed a human shepherd and leader, so a call for help was sent to Buye and the Bishop considered his candidates. Who possessed the faith, love, courage and patience to enable him to face such a situation and then go through with it? He approached Yona and his wife, Mary, and although they had a growing family and Mary was pregnant, they accepted the call.

The story of Yona has been fully written in Dr J. E. Church's moving biography entitled *Forgive Them*,* and the following pages are retold briefly from his book.

His ministry at Maranyundo began with enormous difficulties. He had no house for his wife and family, and was soon seriously ill himself. He needed a permanent helper, so Doreen Peck settled in a small house of her own. Using her car she and Yona visited the sick, battled with a typhoid epidemic, held

* Hodder and Stoughton, London.

open-air meetings, organized schools, interviewed Belgian officials, distributed food and clothing and kept accounts. Yona was entrusted with considerable sums of money from refugee relief funds, from which to buy tons of grain for sowing seeds, banana shoots and coffee plants. Many important representatives from World Refugee Organizations visited him and conferred with him, and when business was over he would say gently, "Now may I give you my testimony, sir?"

God endowed him and Doreen in a very special measure with the spirit of wisdom and understanding, for beside all the planning and administration, he had a big building programme on his hands: the primary school, houses for the staff, himself and Doreen, and finally, the church. All these projects provided work, interest and small earnings for many of the refugees, and a new purpose in life.

But, although he was longing for his family, his own house did not head the list. "Pray for my wife and me," he wrote. "She has not been able to join me for seven months because there was no house for us. But God has led us on and helped us and given us much peace which comes from Calvary."

At last the little home was ready and Mary arrived with the five children, and it was perhaps the testimony of this Christian home as much as anything else, that drew the women to Christ. They flocked round Mary, amazed at the love and respect that Yona showed to his wife. "Do you mean to say he never beats you, never curses you?" they would ask. "No," she would reply. "Sometimes he asks my forgiveness and sometimes I ask his and then we pray about the matter." And the women would wag their heads in speechless amazement.

Another shining testimony was the funeral of their two-year-old baby, Joy, who did not long survive the oppressive, mosquito-ridden climate. Huge crowds attended the burial and Yona turned it into an occasion of triumph. "How can we mourn," he cried, "when God has planned what is best for us and for our little one?" And someone was heard to remark, "Now at last we see a faith that works; that brings comfort in death and sorrow." Through this bitter grief the parents drew closer to their people and were able to enter more deeply into their sorrows and suffering and comfort them from their own experience. So their valley of weeping became a well, and they became gentle, more compassionate, more touched by the infirmities of those about them. When Yona saw people lacking food and clothing, he would go home to Mary and say, "Come and see those whom Jesus spoke about when He said, 'I was hungry and ye did not feed Me, I was naked and ye did not clothe Me,' " and from their own meagre store they would give what they could to help.

The busy, burdened months rolled by. The refugees had built houses and planted gardens and all over the district children were flocking to the schools. There were hundreds of baptisms. Church collections soared and a new spirit of self-help and hope began to pervade the place. By 1963 over six thousand people were receiving instruction, but Yona and Mary were not satisfied. They longed for a deeper work of God and on Easter week-end they planned a conference for women, led by Mr and Mrs Guillebaud and Tabita, Paulo and Dorothy, and African Christian leaders. The meetings were again held under the great acacia tree, and the same theme was "Jesus, the Water of Life". The story of Mara was simply and beautifully told, the tree thrown into the bitter waters; so the bitterness of the refugee camp had been turned to sweetness by the Cross of Jesus. Then, at Whitsun, another team of students from Buye came, led by Alan Lindsay, and through these two conventions, the wind of God's Spirit blew clear and strong, and many were the moving testimonies given by those who had lost all, but had found Christ.

It was like a radiant sunset before the night. Already the land was in an upheaval, owing to the terrorist reprisals aimed at the new Hutu Government. Desperate bands of refugees in exile—the Cockroaches, as they called themselves—had attempted to come back across the borders with the purpose of overthrowing the Republic and re-establishing their own King; and fear of these raiders had bred fresh waves of blind hatred, and all Tutsi were suspect, as were also those who had helped them in their distress. Mass arrests and executions took place, and numbers of others were thrown into prison for no other reason than that they had kept clear of politics, and shared their bread with the hungry. Rumours were afloat that arrests would shortly be made in the Bugesera.

Christmas 1963 was a time of terror, and the Christians packed in and around Yona's house as they were afraid to meet at the church. Yona read the Litany and a great murmur of fervent response went up from the multitude. "From blindness of heart, envy, hatred and malice, and all uncharitableness, Good Lord, deliver us. From lightning and tempest; from battle and murder and sudden death, Good Lord, deliver us." He preached from the final prayer, "And grant that in all our troubles we may put our full trust in Thy mercy," and when he had finished, people began to repent of their fears and to rejoice.

In January, a friend came to him and told him, "You are going to die."

Yona replied, "Why? For what reason am I to die?" Then the person answered, "There are two charges against you. Firstly, because of your stand for the Word of God, and secondly, because you love everyone, indiscriminately."

To which Yona replied, "These two things, the Word of God and the Love of God, are like garments with which God has clothed me and I cannot go without them."

He told Mary about this and they had a time of prayer together, and she remembered his prayer which was something like this, "Oh, God, it was You who called me and sent me to this country. You know about me, the days I have lived and and the days that are left to me. If it is Your Will to call me Home, I leave the decision with You."

On the 4th January another friend came and said to him, "I

have great sadness because you are going to die. They are going to kill you because of your fearless speaking of the Truth and because of your sympathy and love."

Yona replied to him, "I have peace because I know of no reason why I should die. I have not done anyone any harm; I have not treated anyone unfairly. However, if God wants me to go Home by this road, I shall go rejoicing."

Mary and his friends were worried about these threats, but Yona went about his work as usual and did not alter his message. On the 12th January, which was a Sunday, the restrictions were easier, and many people came to church. Yona preached with great power on the text, "Watch, therefore, for ye know neither the day nor the hour."

On the fateful 23rd January, the Rev Ian Leakey, then head of Shyogwe Secondary School, came to visit him and got a great welcome. But as they talked, he realized that Yona was aware of his personal danger, for information had leaked out about a list of victims who were due to be arrested. They prayed, and Yona prayed for the witness of God's people, the leaders of the Roman Catholic and Protestant Churches, and he rejoiced that his home was in Heaven and his life in God's hands. "At 3 p.m. we parted," wrote Ian Leakey, "I shall always remember his strong, radiant smile and the peace of that meeting. He could have come with me, but he chose to stay. His conscience was clear and he refused to leave his place of duty."

After that, Mary takes up the narrative.

"Yona finished his day's work and darkness had fallen about seven-thirty in the evening. We were all sitting in the house when six soldiers came to the door and called for him, saying they had a question to ask him. He opened the door, for they often came to his house by day. But when he had let them in they made a circle around him and said, 'We are going to question you.'

"At this the children and I were filled with grief, and began to cry out to God aloud, saying, 'Oh, God, look upon the injustice of this world of Thine.' We had never before seen Yona surrounded by soldiers at night. That was why we cried out aloud. We knew what a night visit like this meant, for night after night men had been taken away in Jeeps and had never come back.

"Then they took Yona away in the Jeep, but we continued crying out and calling, and Yona asked them to stop the Jeep so that he could go back and comfort his wife and children. They gave permission for this, and he came back to us and said, 'Mary, you know that I honour God and have a clear conscience, so don't worry. I shall come back; it is just some questions they want to ask me.'

"So they took him away and with him, Andrew, the headmaster of the school, but I think at that moment I knew Yona was going to Heaven. . . .''

Little news reached Mary until Saturday when a church teacher appeared with a message from Andrew for her. Andrew himself escaped into Burundi and told the full story to Dr and Mrs Hindley who translated it in the following words:

"Yona died rejoicing. He died praying; praying for those who were going to kill him.

"On Thursday, the 23rd January 1964, at seven o'clock in the evening, a Jeep with six soldiers arrived in front of the pastor's house and he was called outside. He went with a stout heart, trusting God. Two of the soldiers came to my house and told me I was also wanted. I went outside and found my friend, Yona, already there. We went off with a third prisoner towards the town of Kigali, where I thought we were being taken. When Yona saw we were going towards this town, he said to me, 'Let us surrender our lives into God's hands.' He did not say this because of any evil he had done, but because for many days he had seen the soldiers taking people away like this, and they never came back.

"We continued on our way, crossing the river, and a little way on the further side we saw about eight more soldiers. They ordered us out of the Jeep and told us to surrender anything we had. The third prisoner had a small suitcase which he put on the ground, and I put my watch on his case.

"Yona then asked permission to write in his diary, and he wrote, 'We are going to Heaven.' And then added, as carefully as he could in the time, an account of the church francs left in his house. He placed his diary, with the key of his cupboard, on the case, as well as a few francs from his pocket and asked the soldiers to see that his wife was given these things.

"One soldier said, 'You had better pray to your God.' So we all stood up and Yona prayed thus, 'Lord God, You know we have not sinned against the Government, and now I pray You to look upon our innocent blood and help these men who know not what they are doing. In the name of Jesus Christ, our Lord, Amen.'

"Then we were told to sit down and they brought ropes and tied our arms behind our backs. One soldier was told to lead Yona away, but before he went we had sung the hymn which in our books is number 212 and says,

> *There is a happy land,*
> *Far, far away,*
> *Where saints in glory stand,*
> *Bright, bright as day.*

"When we had finished singing, they took him away, and as he went he asked me, 'Do you believe?' and I said, 'Yes, I believe because we read that whosoever believes will be saved.' Then he went, singing,

> *There's a land that is fairer than day,*
> *And by faith we can see it afar,*
> *For the Father waits over the way,*
> *To prepare us a dwelling place there.*

"The soldiers took him back to the bridge over the river. There they shot him and threw his body into the water.

"I was left sitting with the third prisoner and the other soldier. They were all amazed. They had never seen anyone go, singing, to his death or walking as he did—like a man just taking a stroll. The soldiers then called me to them, and I went. They asked me to sit again, and asked me my name, and then they returned my watch to me. I asked them to keep it and send it to my wife, but they ordered me to put it on. Then they put me in the Jeep again, and leaving the third prisoner on the road with some of the soldiers, we returned to the camp. They called at the house of the Roman Catholic headmaster and then told me to go home, adding that if I said a word to anyone about the killing of our pastor I, too, would be killed. God, in His mercy, later sent a man to lead me through the bush, so that I might flee to another country where I have found refuge. . . ."

All over Uganda, and Rwanda and Burundi, men received the words of the missionary radio network with stunned horror. "Yona is dead." From high-up government officials to lowly refugees, they mourned for him as for a beloved friend and father, and not only in East Africa is he loved and remembered. His name has been added to the list of modern martyrs in the Memorial Chapel at St Paul's Cathedral in London, and Andrew's account of his death has been added to their Roll of Honour. But his real memorial lives on in the hearts of thousands of refugees. "At first," they wrote, "we were in deep despair, waiting hourly for death. Then some of us saved people felt rebuked, for although our pastor had been taken from us, the Lord Jesus was still with us and we must continue His work here."

"So", wrote Doreen Peck who had been in England at the time of the murder, "they began to meet together for prayer and praise, and people came to the instruction class. Soon, a message was sent to the nearest pastor to come and baptize new candidates. But from the first they began to pray for another pastor of their own."

And God answered their prayers. In July 1964, Yustasi and his wife, Marion, arrived—faithful, loving shepherds—and the work of blessing and revival went steadily on all over the Bugesera. Truly, the desert had rejoiced and the solitary place had been made glad.

20

Maintaining the Life

I suppose that the main purpose in the writing of this book is to record what God has done through men and women who, in spite of their weakness, mistakes and failures, loved Him, sought to obey Him and humbled themselves under His hand. Within the span of fifty years, the Gospel has flooded a land that was sunk in witchcraft, heathendom and degradation. A living, growing indigenous Church has been established and Christian teaching is being given in many schools and hospitals. In Kigezi, Rwanda and Burundi, the Bible has been translated into three different languages and put into the hands of the whole population.

Perhaps also, in an unprecedented way, God has committed into the hand of this Mission and their converts a secret for which all mankind is searching; an answer to a question that torments every thinking human being today as he remembers the Congo massacres, the torment of Vietnam, Biafra and the Middle East, the unknown horrors of Siberia and Tibet, or the problems of apartheid. There has only, ever, been one answer; and here in Rwanda it has, in a sense, been worked out and demonstrated. It is found in the light that blazed from the life of Jesus, in the love that triumphed at the death of Jesus, and in the life imparted through the resurrection of Jesus.

To stand in that light is to see ourselves against the background of God's holiness and to be broken and humbled. To walk with Jesus is to live in that light, recognizing all our shortcomings. Hatred, pride, superiority and complacency are swept away in the resulting flood of self-hatred. There is nowhere to turn save to that one Refuge for all sinners, the Cross, and here there is no favouritism. Christ as He is lifted up draws us all, and the nearer we draw to Him the nearer we draw to each other. Here is true reality: a sinner exposing himself to the healing, atoning love of the Redeemer and to the cleansing of His blood. Then, by the power of His risen life, he can be filled with that same quality of love that embraces all and denies none, that suffers and sacrifices and redeems. No barriers can stand before such love. It overcomes racial superiority, racial hatred, revenge, fear, misunderstanding and jealousy. It has proved a single, uniting loyalty that overrides all other party loyalties and annuls all other divisions. This was revival and this will always be revival.

But life needs to be maintained and we have the responsibility of co-operating in prayer for this. Life must be maintained first of all in the Church. Today it has African bishops, archdeacons and pastors who are wholly consecrated to God. But it is not easy to rise in the space of two or three decades from the ranks of houseboy and ward orderly to the splendour of office and title, and to rule those who for generations have ruled others. Life shows itself as they walk humbly with God and firmly and righteously before men.

Life must be maintained in the *Balokale*—the revived section of the Church—many of whom are old men and women by now. The language of the Revival will grow meaningless, unless their lives remain radiant and attractive, and they stretch out their hands in loving understanding to bridge the gap that exists between them and the younger generation.

For there is a broad rift which is, perhaps, one of the biggest problems the Church has to contend with. Those who passed through the Revival of the thirties and forties were mostly a rural people with a poorer education and a simpler outlook. They are conservative in dress, and their singing often seems confined to one well-loved chorus which embodies all the sweet memories of the past. Their emphasis is more on fellowship and individual witness than on organized evangelism. On the whole, they look askance at the hundreds of restless, sophisticated, educated young people with their modern clothes and hair styles, who flock into the youth meetings and Scripture Union rallies with guitars and want to set their hymns to African tunes and pop rhythms. Few of the older group have been able to break through to impart the secrets Christ has taught them to the growing generation, and the leadership of the young is mostly in their own hands or in the hands of the foreign missionary who recognizes the pulsating potentiality of this new mission-field, but is often far too busy with other work to do much about it.

It seems fantastic, for instance, that Viera Gray, with the crushing full-time responsibility of Buye Hospital and Nurses' Training School on her shoulders, should also be running the Girls' Brigade; or that Keith Anderson, in the ordinands' training school with his vital task of individual counselling and carefully prepared theological teaching, should have to write, "Struggling with nuts and bolts, oil and grease, wires and fuses, motors and generators, seems to sum up about a quarter of the last eighteen months. Language study, teaching, and the Boys' Brigade make up the rest."

If ever there were "fields ripe for harvest", it is among the youth of Uganda, Rwanda and Burundi, and there is a wide-open door for Scripture Union groups, camps, and Christian Unions. Maureen New writes, "The need to give a sense of direction to youth, apart from school activities, and to provide an outlet for their pent-up energy and enthusiasm, is very acute. 'We want to do something,' is not at all an uncommon outburst. 'Just show us; tell us. Give us books on what to do— anything.' "

A start has been made and a little group are now able to give the matter their whole attention. Mr Kenneth Kitley, visiting the teachers and schoolchildren of Burundi; Festo Kivengere, one of the very few Africans who is effectively managing to pass on the revival message of repentance and reality to enormous crowds of young people; Peter and Elisabeth Guillebaud seconded as Scripture Union workers; Eric and Ruth Townson who have heard God's call to the youth of Rwanda; Pat and Pam Brooks, teaching students in Bujumbura. "We desperately need full-time, ex-patriate youth workers in each country," writes Mr Kitley, "whose responsibility would be to survey the needs at different age levels and to lay the foundations of an approach to these groups. We pray that, even now while waiting the coming of such workers, one or more missionaries may be set free from other work to visit the schools and to start the training of suitable young Christian leaders upon whom all will eventually depend."

Life must be maintained in the schools. Although education has largely come through the Church, they are rapidly being infected by materialism and atheism and there is still plenty of room for the ex-patriate Christian teacher. Many of the original mission schools are now having to employ unbelieving—or even immoral—teachers, and it is a hard life. Young Africa demands more and more, and is less and less content with what the present educational system can give. In the boys' secondary schools strikes and riots are not unknown. But there is still freedom for Bible teaching, and above all, for the witness of a consistent life.

When a boy's behaviour proved so irritating that even Mabel Jones' patience broke down, she apologized to him. Later on in the day she received a little note from him asking if he could speak to her. "I have come to you", he said quietly, "because I have a problem. When you get angry, you know what to do, but when I get angry I do not know what to do."

Life must be maintained in the hospitals, so that their true function of healing and leading people to Christ may be fulfilled. There are young doctors bearing medical, surgical, spiritual, administrative and financial responsibilities far beyond their years. The doctor on call twenty-four hours a day, or the nurse having to do a doctor's work as well as her own when there is no doctor available, has little left to give, physically or mentally, to the spiritual side of the work.

And life must be maintained in the missionaries. There is still a place for those who are willing to go and put their gifts and training at the disposal of the African Church—not as leaders, but as helpers and sharers. The situation demands a high degree of humility, loyalty and adaptability; for the time may come soon when foreigners will no longer be needed. But at present the Church still welcomes youth-workers, teachers, doctors, nurses, agriculturists and those able to teach trades, and the whole structure could not exist without them.

The older missionaries—fathers and shepherds of the flock have seen and have rejoiced in the wonderful things God has done. But they are not immune from Satan's attacks. No one can live on a past experience and apart from Jesus, that Rock on whom they are so firmly grounded, they will fail as easily as the newest convert.

Among the younger missionaries there are many who find their work satisfying and rewarding; but there are some, too, who are struggling with depression and disappointment. For the young wives, the burden of loneliness and homesickness perhaps falls heavier than on any others. On the whole, the young wife is as capable and qualified as the unmarried woman submerged in her job, but for years she may have to stay at home, tied to her small children. Shops, if there are any, hold few attractions and there may be no other young European wives to chat with. At first, language is a barrier to her having much fellowship with local African wives. Her husband is probably doing the work of several men and may, or may not, appear before late at night, and then so dead with weariness or so bowed down with his own problems that relaxing conversation may be difficult.

What is the remedy? I do not pretend to know, except the

realization of the incalculable importance of the first years of a little child's life and of the value of a man's home. The final responsibility for the organization of the local work, and the settlement of delicate relationships requiring a deep knowledge of the African, may rest on the inexperienced shoulders of one young man and may threaten to engulf him. His wife may be his chief counsellor, his home his only refuge, and all honour to the woman who can so conquer her own frustrations, depression and homesickness, that when her husband pops in for a hurried meal at the wrong time, and pops out again to do a major emergency operation, she can be at leisure from herself to listen to his problems. Many a young missionary would have cracked if it had not been for the peace of his home and for the understanding and courage of his wife; but it needs a self-forgetfulness and dedication to God's work as deep as that of anyone.

It is much harder to be than to do, and this was once well expressed by Dr Algie Stanley Smith in a letter to a new young missionary, a letter she has treasured for many years: "And now all the years of preparation are over and you are on the threshold of what, I trust, will be your lifework. I know the Lord has been teaching you lessons which will have prepared you for much of what lies ahead, but in the real event it isn't the lessons learnt which will help you; it is only Jesus realized, lived with moment by moment and obeyed. He must take you in hand from the word 'Go', and do His work in you. I believe that what He does in us and for us is far more important than the actual work we do. It is what we are that counts, and if we are to be of any use, it is just Jesus living in us, so our chief preoccupation must be Him."

Some new missionaries undergo a reaction of disillusionment and disappointment because they have read about the revival and now—"Where is it?" Apart from a very few transformed lives, all they see, at first, is suspicion, division and materialism.

234

Revival is still going on, and probably more in those districts where there is no missionary than at the mission centres. Right up to date, waves of revival have been sweeping through a number of secondary boarding schools and out from them to hospitals and the people around. It is notable that it is specially the educated young people who are being saved. A missionary nurse writes:

"One night we heard the sound of singing coming across from the school hill. The girls often sang but this sounded different from those other times. They sounded full of praise and joy and even from the distance one realized that the Lord was working. The next night the same thing happened and we could hear their singing going on. We were filled with curiosity and many of the hospital workers went over to investigate. What met our eyes as we entered into the school dining-room where the girls were meeting, was an amazing sight. People were repenting of deep things, especially of hatred for one another. As one girl stood up to say what the Lord had said to her, the rest of the girls burst out into songs of praise and joy to the Lord. They clapped and danced their joy and it all seemed so natural. Then they quietly sat down as another spoke. It was the most thrilling meeting I have ever been to.

"Some youths appeared in the meeting and a few of them stood up in the midst of great jubilation and confessed that they had come out of curiosity and to laugh and jeer at what was going on, but the Lord met with them and showed them their need of Him. They saw that without Christ, life had no meaning. Some nurses asked forgiveness for laziness in their work and are now working with real zeal and helping their seniors in hospital, and loving the patients and telling them about their Saviour. Of course, they are not little angels all of a sudden, but what a change one can see in them! Others were convicted about stealing hospital things and medicines, and they came to repay what they had taken.

"Every night now a meeting is held in hospital and people

from all around the hill, even the local shops, have been coming along and the Lord has met with them and saved them."

It may be that God does not intend to keep on working to the old pattern. When the Holy Spirit came down in power on East Africa, the Africans were still a young race emerging from paganism, and in times of emotion we tend to revert to type. Dancing and frenzy was still their most familiar mode of expression, and one cannot help feeling that the Lord was far less concerned about this than the missionary was. When we come home to our little children after a long absence, we are not unduly upset if temporarily they lose control of themselves— shout for joy and rush about—although onlookers may remark coldly that we have a very unruly family. But the rather trying behaviour at the moment of meeting does not express the reality of the relationship; that may not come till later when, tired out with all the excitement, the child nestles up to his mother in the dark and realizes that the homesick days are over and that she has really come home. So the ecstacies and disturbances passed quickly, and in the silence and solitude that followed, these Africans knew that God's love had reached them in Christ. Thirty years later many faces still light up with inexpressible joy as they speak of that moment, as though that dawn breaks afresh each time they voice their simple experience, "Jesus came to me."

Africa is no longer in its pagan childhood. The continent has speeded its adolescence and is quickly growing into strong, self-reliant manhood, and the deepest experiences of adolescence usually come without outward manifestation. Revival is not dependent on this. It comes whenever the ordinary Christian, whether he be established saint or tired, discouraged young missionary, looks away from the disillusionment and disappointment and makes contact with Jesus at the deepest level of his life; hears His voice and obeys, and keeps on obeying. This is revival, for at that point the Holy Spirit takes over. "Our cause is never more in danger," says the "enemy of souls" in C. S. Lewis's *Screwtape Letters*, "than when a man, no longer desiring, but still intending to do the Will of God, looks round on the Universe from which all trace of Him seems to have vanished, feels himself forsaken, and still obeys."

And there is no cause for depression. God has ordained that "summer and winter, seedtime and harvest, day and night shall not cease", and in the natural course of events there are two months' harvest in the year. The granite soil of paganism has been broken up by the power of God and the labours of the pioneers, and a tremendous spiritual harvest has been reaped. The soil is now warm and fertile and it is during the ploughing season that a man's muscles develop and he sows his seed in faith and hope. He learns patience through the winter storms, when he goes his way and the seed springs up. He will need all he learned in the waiting season, when the busy, exhausting days of reaping are upon him. If the conditions of God's promises are fulfilled, there will certainly be a harvest; but let us remember, too, in this age of luxury and self-indulgence, that God's prices have not come down. The pioneers paid for revival with their toil and sweat, their anguish and repentance, their prayers, fasting and self-denial, and we shall never have it at a cheaper rate.

But still today men are coming to hear the Word of God; coming down from the red dust roads, over the mountains, through the bush and jungle, along the shores of the lakes or the streets of the new cities. They are coming from the towns, from the kraals, from the banana groves. Wherever God's Word is being preached, they are flocking to hear; into the simple brick churches set on the hills, or to the round, thatched huts where men gather to pray; into the rough schoolrooms with their stained walls; into roofless stockades and crowded hospital wards. The sight of such a multitude might appal us into doing nothing, or cause us to rush into frenzied activities.

"Somewhere we read the other day," wrote Dr Moynagh while still in Africa, "that the greatest competitor for single-

hearted devotion to Jesus is service for Him. As we dream and
think of the future of this country, with its dense population
passing, for the most part, from paganism into Roman Catholic-
ism; as we think of the thousands of children crying out for
education, and of the other thousands, partly educated, crying
out for literature; as we look a little apprehensively across the
borders of this quiet country to troubled areas in Kenya, restlessness in Uganda and closing doors in the Sudan, it would be
easy for us to get worked up into a frenzy of service. We would
despair if we looked at our few numbers and feeble strength,
but we see Jesus, walking over these hills and along the valleys,
knocking patiently at the doors of sin that shut Him out,
sitting down in the Bethany homes of those who love Him,
asking His Father for the heathen for His inheritance and
receiving His answer in redeemed men and women."